Dr. Clarensau has done it again .
effective pastor, combined it with
churches to see turn-around growth, and then added his insightful
research on healthy churches to give us thirty-seven brilliant suggestions
on what people want to know before being led to change. As you read this
book, you will discover the amazing potential that it has just on the other
side of working out these nuggets. Enjoy your journey through this book.

—Doug Clay, General Superintendent for
the Assemblies of God, USA

Most of the books I have read on the subject of "change" have postured
one party's promoting the necessity of change in conflict with another
party's resisting change. In his book, *Subject to Change: What People Want
Their Pastor to Know Before Asking Them to Change*, Dr. Clarensau challenges church leaders who desperately want change to occur and church
members who appear reluctant to change to begin a journey, to find value
in each other's positions and join together for mutual benefit. I wish I
had known the principles he outlines in this book during the four major
ministerial transitions I experienced. Dr. Clarensau offers an approach
to a "change process" that will result in positive outcomes which can be
achieved peaceably without creating "winners and losers." As he concludes
the book, he states, "Healthy churches find healthy paths when they're
pursuing change, and that's the real goal, isn't it? I mean, if you get to
the future and have no one to share it with or have strewn the road with
broken relationships along the way, will it really be the future you want?"

—Alton Garrison, Executive Director, Acts 2 Journey, Former
Assistant General Superintendent for the Assemblies of God, USA

I have watched Mike love God's people unswervingly as a pastor, denominational leader, college dean, and an effective consultant. His dedication
to those the Apostle Paul called "saints" has only grown deeper and richer
with time. I'm thankful Mike distilled into these pages what I've seen

him live through the years of our friendship. Turn each page and you will experience an inverted, insightful, humorous, honest perspective from which every leader in any size church will benefit. When you reach the last page, (and I hope you devour every line!) you will know what I have known for more than three decades: Mike doesn't love the people of God because his job depends on it. He loves the people of God because Jesus loves and believes in them. If we apply these "apples of gold in settings of silver" we will love and lead the people of God even better!

—Dr. Terry L. Yancey, Assemblies of God Kansas (AGK) Ministry Network Superintendent and South Central Region Executive Presbyter for the Assemblies of God, USA

In *Subject to Change*, Dr. Mike Clarensau provides a refreshing, practical and very readable book on the subject of change. Using engaging anecdotes spun with facts and knowledge obtained through a lifetime of effective change leadership, Clarensau empowers leaders to eavesdrop on the thoughts and experiences of the people they are hoping to lead through change. The result will be the discovery of a hope filled pathway through the necessary shifts and adjustments every church community must make to continue to faithfully be with Jesus on His Mission.

—Steven M. Pike, Author of *Next Wave: Discovering the Twenty First Century Church*, Founder, Church Multiplication Network, Next Wave Community, and Urban Islands Project

It is often stated and discussed at length, that leading change is the greatest challenge church leaders face. However, in my twenty-four years of leading a local church and more than a decade of leading a network of over 150 churches, I have never heard anyone address the challenge of being led through change. From his years of research and experience, using his great wisdom and occasional wit, Dr. Mike Clarensau has surfaced a significant truth that church leaders may have overlooked: If we are going to constructively lead change, maybe we should consider how it feels to be asked to change. Across these pages, there are lessons to be learned by both the leader and those being led. Dr. Clarensau has once again brought a very practical tool to the local church to assist them on their journey to God's preferred future. *Subject to Change* has renewed my faith in the great people who make up our churches, as well as in the belief that healthy change can occur. I believe everyone involved in implementing change in the local church should read and glean from the wisdom found in this timely work.

—Thomas Moore, West Florida Ministry Network
Superintendent for the Assemblies of God

OTHER BOOKS BY
MIKE CLARENSAU

A Spirit-Empowered Life: Discover the World-Changing Journey God Has Designed for You. Springfield, MO: Vital Resources, 2015.

From Belonging to Becoming: Learning to Love the Way Jesus Did. Springfield, MO: Influence Resources, 2011.

Clarensau, Mike and Hayes, Clancy. *Give Them What They Want: Turning Sunday School into a Place Where People Want to Be.* Springfield, MO: Gospel Publishing House, 2001.

Journey to Integrity. Springfield, MO: Gospel Publishing House, 1997; 2003 (2nd printing).

The Sanctity of Life. Springfield, MO: Gospel Publishing House, 1996.

We Build People: Making Disciples for the 21st Century. Springfield, MO: Gospel Publishing House, 1996.

Your New Life in Christ: A Twelve-Week Self-Study on Basic Bible Doctrines. Springfield, MO: Gospel Publishing House, 1991; 2004 (4th printing).

MIKE CLARENSAU

SUBJECT TO
CHANGE

WHAT PEOPLE WANT THEIR PASTOR TO KNOW
BEFORE ASKING THEM TO CHANGE

ARROWS &
STONES

DEDICATION

This book is dedicated to deacons, elders, and congregational leaders everywhere. These men and women faithfully prioritize their local church by stepping up to serve and giving hours, even years of their lives to making sure the work of God continues and even advances on their corner.

My dad was one of those. For more than three decades he and my mom lived out their Christianity from the various leadership posts their congregational friends asked them to fill. I watched and took to heart the values that drove them. Today, I get to sit amidst piles of grateful expressions and statements of their influence that remind me that these are people who make the lasting difference. Pastors like me often come and go in the life of a congregation, but it's these kinds of servants—the ones who stay—who truly establish a local church's impact on its community.

I am grateful for every deacon and every elder with whom I've been blessed to serve. Each longed to see our congregation reach its greatest potential. I've met hundreds more in my travels who seem cut from the same cloth. These are the friends who, after forty or more hours of putting bread on their family tables each week, roll up their sleeves and give their best to Christ's mission. I get to lead them.

But I've found I do that best when I listen to them.

ACKNOWLEDGMENTS

Given that this book covers things people have taught me over a couple of decades of leading them and listening to them, thanking all involved likely goes beyond what my memory can achieve or these pages can contain. But that doesn't mean I won't try. . . .

From Ray Rogers and the Schmidly men at my first local church assignment to those who've served my home church and known me my whole life; to Carey, Lyle, Michael, Bill, and John who prayed with me before dawn every Friday morning and trusted me as a rookie pastor; to all those who stood by me as God built a great church around us in Wichita; to all the men and women I've met traveling to hundreds of the congregations where they serve; and all those I've yet to meet as this journey of encouraging local churches continues ahead of me—for all these I say thank you for the insights and the wisdom you've shared with me. I hope I've passed along some of it in these pages.

I'm also grateful to the hundreds of pastors who have trusted me enough to let me walk beside them for a bit of their journeys and meet the friends that walk with them every day. Watching the ways you care for each other and work tirelessly together, has enriched my understanding of what Jesus' Church is divinely designed to be.

Of course, there are those who've helped this book get beyond my notes and into your hands. Over the decade it's taken to compile what you'll read, three different administrative assistants—Samantha, Kristen, and Bailey—have all had a hand in helping me edit these pages. Martyn, Caroline, and the whole team at Four Rivers Media then took things from there.

Finally, I want to thank my wife, Kerry. For nearly four decades now we have chased God's purposes together and encouraged each other down the unique paths He has opened before each of us. This book, and the years and miles it took for me to learn its lessons, didn't happen without her sincere support and sacrifice.

CONTENTS

INTRODUCTION

PERCEPTION . . .

I peeked behind the curtain. . . .

N o, this is not a confession of some sort of voyeuristic escapade. I'm a Midwesterner, and peeking behind the curtain is a euphemism for uncovering the real story—seeing what's happening beyond what's visible—cracking the code to see how things work. Maybe we're too curious. Maybe we're too suspicious. Maybe it's just really hard to impress us.

You might remember my fellow Kansan, Dorothy. She was a peeker, too. Standing amidst an overpowering display in the throne room of the Great and Powerful Oz, Dorothy—in true Midwesterner form—pulled back the curtain to find the real story. Okay—actually, she was trying to find her dog, Toto, who had initiated his own journey of curiosity. Still, Dorothy overcame her own timidity with a desperate desire to get back home with her dog in her arms, and suddenly she found herself staring at the real story behind the amazing Oz. A small, balding, somewhat chubby man, pushing buttons and pulling levers, was speaking into a microphone that seemed larger than his own head. In that moment, Dorothy uncovered for all of us one of life's great truths—add a little reverb and you can sound all-powerful!

Now, let me get back to the curtain I tugged on. Dorothy was disappointed in what she saw, but not me. I was only surprised. Like Auntie Em's favorite niece, I had been prepared to see something, but what I saw turned out to be something else entirely. However, what I saw behind my curtain turned out to be a good thing—a really good thing.

You see, I've attended numerous pastors' conferences, drained thousands of coffee cups with my fellow pulpiteers, and listened to the dreams of hundreds of would-be world changers. I love their passion, their hope, and their determination to make a difference. I'm drawn to such conversations because something like that beats inside of me too.

But quite often, their stories don't come true—at least not on their preferred timetables. Why? Some pastors describe a resistance to their efforts, like an evil Empire that wars against their Jedi skills; they often paint these epic stories using less-than-flattering earth tones:

"You wouldn't believe this *one guy* I have to deal with...."

"I can't get anything done because of a couple of ladies who ..."

"I have a great plan to grow an amazing church and truly impact our town, but *they* ..."

These, they say, are the enemies of change, the status quo protectors gathered around deacon room tables or carrying casserole dishes into potluck dinners. "Don't trust their pleasant smiles, 'cause these folks have a host of flying monkeys at their command." I've heard the scowling faces of "future preventers" described in such wrinkled detail that I had envisioned Frankenstein-like veins popping from their foreheads. I've been left to wonder if those flying monkeys might lead me to the carcass of the previous pastor, 'cause I heard they ate him alive.

Churches don't change because the people won't let them change!

Then I pulled back the curtain. . . .

Actually, there's no real curtain, but I began working with churches and the people inside them. I started sitting at their tables, listening to their attitudes, and helping them scour the challenges they confront. Surprisingly, I saw very few of those popping veins. Instead, I encountered passionate people, some of whom were even desperate to see a new day for their church. I met folks who wanted to reach their communities every bit as much as the pastor who led them. I encountered people who were waiting for some powerful character to pull the right lever for them, and they seemed quite ready to click their ruby red dress shoes together to get there. I still haven't found any evidence of flying monkeys.

More often than not, the portrait of control-freak deacon or stern church matriarch proves a bit overstated. Sure, there are a few such characters out there; but most of them aren't out to control the church. (And yes, I can hear your heart beating faster as you're ready to insist that I don't know the guy *you're* dealing with. It's true, I don't.) It's just that, in these battles, there may be a bit more misunderstanding of those on the other side than we have realized. Many of these congregational dominators have simply felt it necessary to exert a bit more effort to make sure that some painful and confusing event that occurred a while back never happens to them or their church again. Many instances of congregational control turned out to be reactions to "that one time," years ago, when their pastor lost control (but I'll talk about that later).

So our impatience and our people's caution mix to create a volatile brew: the kind that can have your eyes playing tricks on you.

I discovered that the stories, much like Oz's frightening head, had been a bit embellished for effect. No, my pastor friends weren't lying (and neither was I when it was my turn to talk)—it's just that many of us hadn't figured out how to lead these folks effectively yet. Turning them into massive green heads with other Martian-like features made the intended lessons of our tales easier to grasp. The truth—that we stepped into a story we didn't start and found ourselves struggling with our willingness to invest the kind of time it would take to really catch up—doesn't extract as much pity. So our impatience and our people's caution mix to create a volatile brew: the kind that can have your eyes playing tricks on you.

It turns out that most church members are really good people who want really good things for their church—even "God things." Most of them can quote the Great Commission and they *really want to live it*. It's just that, when you live in the passenger seat and you've been going in circles for a while, it's hard not to comment on the latest turn…especially when the road looks too familiar. The more I learn, the harder it is to blame them. Still, I can also understand why their expressions of doubt—their stomping on imaginary brakes—might irritate the current driver.

The point is that these are good folks and they need to be led into the future more effectively. So, in these pages about leading change, I'm going to describe change from the passenger seat, discover what we can learn from that side of the windshield, and maybe find fresh insights into how pastor and people can get where we *both* really want to go—together. I've called this book *Subject to Change* because that's what many congregations are. They are subject to our repeated, and occasionally clumsy, efforts to bring change to their world.

But first, I must confess my Dorothy-ness. I'm a pastor and, like that pig-tailed traveler, there's somewhere I want to go. I've sat in the congregational driver's seat and jingled the keys between my fingers. But I've also listened to and learned from hundreds of church members, and I know they want to do more than control the car stereo. I know these so-called "laypeople" don't just want to "lay" there. In fact, I've come to respect them and I love the passion I see in a great many of them. So I don't really want to take sides.

Instead, I want to move forward—to travel with anyone who's looking for yellow bricks to journey on. I'm quite aware of the critical need for change in thousands of churches. Currently, I board a plane every week to work with such folks in their pursuit of a new day. And ultimately, I want to help you get wherever "there" is for your church and discover the goodness in those who travel at your side—those on the receiving end of your search for a new day or those who, like you, are subject to change.

CHAPTER ONE

PASSION . . .

My family didn't raise sheep. . . .

'm a city kid with a farm heritage. Mom's folks were small-operation dairy farmers, an ancestry that landed me in fields and barns four to six times each year. To say that I didn't really fit the rural mold would make my cousins chuckle. I was a bookworm with a preferred television schedule. They enthusiastically pulled on those udders when grandpa offered us an adventure in his livelihood. I remain convinced that Bessie didn't want me touching her there.

But, while environs where cats only exist for mice and yard games requiring a heightened manure awareness helped shape my childhood, we didn't raise sheep. Instead, my knowledge of Mary's lamb and whatever family he might have abandoned to tag along on that freckled girl's journey has come from books—clean, fragrant pages with cute pictures and smile-inducing paragraphs. My sheep study has never required me to leave my boots outside or test a detergent's capacity for eliminating odors.

It seems sheep are a challenging lot—at least from what I've read.

Many insist that those grass-eating, sweater-makers lack intelligence, a judgment based mostly on their apparent willingness to go where others go, regardless of the destination. I hear they smell, can't clean themselves, and manage to get themselves in the most awkward jams, necessitating the rescue of a loving shepherd. Their single-syllable vocabularies have them sounding like the irritated noises my uncle used to make when he left his footprint in the . . . uh . . . when he needed to leave his boots outside. There's nothing very attractive about sheep—at least not about the real ones, who never pose for storybook photos.

So forgive my surprise in realizing that these ignorant fuzz balls manage to procure significant screen time in Bible stories. In fact, they seem to be Jesus' analogy of choice when describing our connection to Him. We're the sheep to His shepherd—a comparison that captures both our waywardness and His extraordinary dedication. I may not relish the implications of ignorance, but I'll gladly lay down my defensiveness if it means we get a shepherd like that. I'll hum along with David's tunes about green pastures and still waters. I'll admit to my sheep-like stupidity if it means that Jesus will return to the sheepfold with me draped across His shoulders. So, for the remaining balance of the Church Age, sheep pictures will adorn Sunday school classrooms like spiritual selfies with Jesus joining us in the frame.

But if you move Jesus too far from the story, the whole sheep idea stinks. If you replace Him with one of his trainees—a staff-wielding grass-chaser who still smells a bit like his last flock—I'm done reading the sheep lines in this drama. Jesus as shepherd makes a great story. Pastors in that role can be a mixed experience. They're usually sincere and sing David's songs on key, but they can't always keep their own wool from protruding over their collars. Yet this is the arrangement even Jesus seemed to want as He relaunched a failing fisherman into a new line of work: "Peter, feed my sheep."

The subsequent relationships between sheep and shepherd, congregation and pastor, haven't always matched the picture. Sheep aren't always as spotless and "pet-able" as the paintings suggest, and shepherds have been known to use their curl-handled lumber as more than a walking stick. While some such pairs achieve a healthy coexistence—even a life-changing friendship that offers future generations of sheep some real hope—piles of tattered wool and the smell of lamb chops show us that this relationship can be difficult.

And when it comes to leading change, more than a few shepherds have come in from the fields bleeding. Apparently, sheep bite. At the same time, some parishioners can show their own wounds from a change journey. It seems that a few shepherds aren't afraid to leave their most disagreeable charges tied to the occasional wilderness tree. *Baaa*, indeed!

The slightly ornery phrasing of this book's subtitle suggests that we're headed toward a concrete list of specific and, hopefully helpful, ideas. "What Church People Want Their Pastor to Know Before Asking Them to Change" implies that those in the pew have some real input to offer to their shepherd—a reality I have discovered to be true again and again.

The first of these unexpected insights is that *we may not want the same things*.

What do you suppose sheep want in a shepherd relationship? Now, I realize that nobody really asks such questions of barnyard animals, partly because of the single-syllable vocabularies we've already mentioned and partly because talking to animals is one childhood dream that can end in adulthood admittance to a psychiatric ward. If sheep are answering your questions, farming may not be for you.

But if we could coil ourselves inside the tiny cubbyhole where a sheep's intellect quietly dwells, what would we learn about their goals for their shepherd? My guess would be that green grass and quiet streams where the current doesn't threaten to topple you off of your lamb legs would top the list. "Take care of us," is the most likely translation of that *Baaa* sound.

Good shepherds oblige, but they often have a different set of goals. They want to preserve the sheep, helping them grow healthy while somehow maintaining their spotlessness; but they also want to grow the flock. Bigger flocks often indicate better shepherds. Old Testament stories show Abraham, nephew Lot, son Isaac, and even grandson Jacob establishing their wealth through sheep multiplication. But sheep and shepherd pursuing different passions in the midst of their relationship can create some challenges. I'm guessing that sheep don't typically mind having more sheep around, provided the grass and water are abundant. Still, it's likely that the shepherd celebrates new members of the flock a little more exuberantly. Sheep don't throw baby showers.

When we trade the barnyard for the sanctuary, this potential disconnect comes into practical focus. Not long ago, I met with the leadership team of a smaller congregation as they were preparing to welcome their new pastor. I had spoken with the new "shepherd" a few days earlier and I marveled at his excitement, knowing that his most recent predecessors in this role had struggled a great deal. History wasn't really on his side, but his dream of building a great church and reaching his community in creative ways was captivating. *Maybe he's the one*, I told myself. Like Yoda and the other Jedi masters around the presbytery table, I wanted to believe that balance might have come to their Force.

Problem is, the people had a different agenda. Yes, they wanted to experience God's future and see their church reach the full potential that their founders had dreamed about and prayed for since half a century ago. These are good people who would never say "No" to the Great Commission. But I knew that their enthusiasm for this moment of decision centered on having a pastor, a shepherd, one who would care for them and nourish them from God's Word. They treasured what is and what had been, while *his* eyes searched elsewhere for what could be. And in a matter of minutes, I could see that their enthusiasms weren't for the same path.

Here's the first intersection of change and trouble. Pastor and people try to imagine they're on the same road when they're actually seeking different destinations. He dreams of larger flocks and producing enough wool to warm the entire village. They long for greener grass and cool, refreshing drinks at crystal pools. He pleads with them to help him chase down more sheep, and they beg him not to forget that they're sheep too.

Truth is, they're both right. Jesus' clear vision for His Church is ever expanding, seeking to fulfill His Commission within its community and beyond, and at the same time it's all about loving one another, nourishing each other with His wisdom, and caring for every little lamb with a need. Sadly, the pastor and the people seemed to each have a different half of the playbook. Two very different goals, two remarkably distinct directions, and two agendas that often bring a confusing "why" to the issue of change.

> ## Pastor and people try to imagine they're on the same road when they're actually seeking different destinations.

Now, the danger in identifying these two conflicting ideas is in accusations of mutual exclusivity. Pastors with their eyes on church growth aren't calloused to or disinterested in the needs of the existing congregation. Such an assumption would be unfair. And it would be just as careless to imply that the congregation is so consumer-driven that they don't really care about anyone else's healthy life plan or eternal hotel reservations.

Yet, when there is change conflict in a church, those are often the colors chosen with which to paint one another into corners. And suddenly, it seems that the amps have been shut off, turning Jesus' command to love one another into little more than a faint whisper. . . .

"Pastor doesn't care about us . . . he's only interested in new people. . . ."

"Those people have no concern for others . . . they just want to control everything and make sure it continues to be the way they like it. . . ."

"Pastor's just trying to make a name for himself so some bigger church will call him and pay him more money. . . ."

"No wonder the last pastor left. These people have no vision at all. . . ."

Here's where that whole "peeking behind the curtain" episode proves so important. These statements, no matter how they might be buttressed by anecdotal stories and the kind of undeniable evidence that makes your friends think you have an open-and-shut case, are simply not true.

Pastors *do* care, though they may feel overwhelmed by what seems to be an endless set of congregational expectations. Ministering to people like you is the core motivation that led them to choose this life path in the first place. I've met hundreds of pastors—maybe even thousands—and have yet to encounter one that I'd feel comfortable insisting is little more than an empire builder.

And here's something pastors need to know. Your people *do* love others and want to see them come to faith. They do want their church to excel at affecting your community, and they long for their efforts under your banner to fuel their own reason-for-being. They've processed dozens of sermons and have been challenged with the mission—the same mission that brought you to their little town—so often that they feel defeated by the gap between where they are and where they're convinced God wants them to be. Don't write them off or toss them onto a pile that's carelessly labeled.

They want what you want.

When I became pastor of Maranatha Worship Center in Wichita, Kansas in the late summer of 2000, twelve 8 x 10 framed photos greeted me as I walked through the church hallway. These were my ancestors in the role of congregational shepherd. Their pictures, and the nameplates that reminded viewers of their tenure, served as the remaining evidence of their sweat and toil, encased in $5 frames. I made a mental note to have my picture taken. I was pastor number thirteen—an apparent tribute to my good fortune, as I assumed the leadership chair in this church's

78th year. The current label was the church's third name, the building its third location, and the somewhat stern faces of my dozen predecessors reminded me that this had been their journey before it became mine.

But it wasn't their faces that motivated me. Within a month, I had removed the 8 x 10s, combining these historical headshots into a single collage with a $40 frame. Now, they all stared at me together, and some of their eyes seemed to follow me ... but their faces and their dreams didn't generate my marching orders.

Honestly, it wasn't a large—and somewhat awkward—painting of Jesus that drove me, either. Yes, it's His Church and His Commission and His Kingdom. In fact, everything of consequence in that place was and still is His. It's just that I discovered that Jesus and me weren't playing on some exclusive team on that Wichita corner. He'd recruited a lot of other teammates to our effort.

They were my motivation. In my first months on the ecclesiastical job, I met the lambs I was assigned to feed. Some had been in the flock a long time, those who still had First Assembly of God bumper stickers on their cars—a reminder of what the sign at the previous location had said. A handful could remember the days of Pentecostal Tabernacle, the church's first identity, more than a decade before the Great Depression disrupted their teen years. This was the congregation I came to pastor, even though no one had hung their pictures in the hallway.

Twelve pastors, twelve visions, twelve new days and new dreams had each taken their turn in the big chair over the decades, but it was the people who remained. And while their collective sense of direction seemed to need a new compass and their current hymn preferences preferred a language no longer sung or spoken, they still possessed a distinct and clear heartbeat. Those graying and balding heads nodded with firm affirmation that a passion for Christ's work still pounded in their hearts—a passion nurtured by God relationships that had celebrated many anniversaries.

And that's the second thing people wish their pastor knew about leading them in change—*they really want the same thing you do, even if they might want it for different reasons.*

_____

My eldest granddaughter is now a beautiful young woman. Several years ago, she hovered at the midpoint between her third and fourth birthdays. We were just a few months from heading to Disneyland for a first princess adventure—the natural result of DVDs watched and dolls purchased over the past forty months. Now, understand that my granddaughter is perfect—I'd just like to get that out there. But in those days, on occasion, she could become upset for reasons her Papa Mike proved unable to discern. We might have been playing on her swing set or imagining that we were battling sharks and whales from the sofa boat in her living room, when suddenly, I was found to be paddling the wrong way or not doing something else right. In that moment, her arms crossed in irritation and the tears that burst forth (hers) were quite real. Soon, she was off to tell her mom that I'd nearly crashed our imaginary boat or that I'd left our mermaid friends behind.

They really want the same thing you do, even if they might want it for different reasons.

I'd thought my daughter-in-law changed the subject when she asked my little blonde princess a funny question: "Do you need a cheese stick?" The blonde head nodded, consumed the snack, and within minutes, our boat was back on course for fun in the imaginary sun. How? Uh . . . *what*? I was confused, but I just kept paddling. Clearly, my daughter-in-law was a toddler whisperer. Later, my wife explained that the episode of frustrated tears was brought on by hunger. Apparently the scientific word is "hangry," and the solution is a healthy snack. I didn't understand because there was nothing in the emotional buildup to connect my errant paddling with the need for a protein-laden cheese stick.

When pastors and congregations begin their journey together, there's so much they don't understand about each other. Pastor encounters reactions to his well-intended steps that seem out of place or hard to understand. He doesn't know the reality behind the reaction so he sits in his sofa boat, feeling perplexed and more than a little misunderstood. He doesn't know the *why* of such moments and there aren't any cheese sticks in the church refrigerator.

As we have said, this relationship likely started with somewhat different goals—pastor wants to build a great church and the people want to have a great pastor. And when their reactions to one another are difficult to understand, the tendency is to fill in the blanks with what we assume the other is feeling.

So they're against my efforts . . . becomes *They're opposed to God's real purposes* . . . becomes *They don't really want me to be their pastor* . . . becomes *They can leave if they want to*—and somebody usually does.

But what is really going on?

First, I know a few things: my granddaughter loves me, she loves to play sofa boat, and my steering away from sharks and rescuing mermaids on the high seas will often earn me a hero's reward (a high five, a hug, and an adorable giggle). And, pastor, your congregation wants to win with you, too. They desperately want you to be successful in steering their journey and rescuing their future. They chose you or welcomed your denomination's choice of you because, on some level, you represent what they want to be. Why else would aging congregations have a younger pastor? Why else would troubled churches prioritize the wisdom of an experienced shepherd? At this juncture in the journey, they need what you are, even if they're acting a bit "hangry" at the congregational meetings.

Here's where the pastor-people relationship can jump the rails before the train barely gets going. Pastor, if you misinterpret behavior and miss your congregation's genuine passion, you'll be tempted to abandon the sofa boat—or at least refuse to play until everyone promises never to cry. If I did that with my beautiful granddaughter, imagine what I would miss. How sad to allow such an important relationship to deteriorate when all you really lacked was a small dairy product.

Second, loving my granddaughter is more critical than rescuing mermaids. Now, I don't mean to compare the vital ministries of the Church with a game conceived in the imagination of a toddler, but loving my little blonde princess is what the whole sofa boat game is about, and loving each other is really the whole ballgame at church, too.

I can almost hear your heart rate accelerate as you grasp a few reasons to resist that last sentence, but the Savior who elevated "love one another" to the top of our list would agree with me. So would the students who fought grass stains to sit at His feet. They underscored His priority by passing along the news that our love for each other was the only thing that would help folks connect the dots between us and Him. Another wise fellow came along a bit later to tell us that all of our well-intended ministry efforts would either be worthless noise or of no value whatsoever without the key ingredient of love. So the change journey that might lie ahead of us can't sidestep the fact that how well we love each other is the *most important item* on our report card. If you get an "A" in achievement and a "D" in love, the parent-teacher conference with your Heavenly Father isn't going to go well (especially since He's both parent and teacher).

Third, *don't assume that our resistance to your new ideas means we're just attached to the status quo.* Your congregation can see what hasn't been working. While they may resist new ideas in favor of the old, they aren't holding out for an imaginary world where they can just paddle their boats through yesterday's familiar ruts to nowhere. It's just that, in most cases, the status quo used to work.

I searched my congregation's history for any sign of an official decision to become ineffective. Because older churches tend to prioritize their historical documents a bit more than what might be healthy, I had access to everything I needed for such a research project. I read about necessary plumbing projects and close votes on vehicle purchases, but nowhere was a motion made to add ineffective ministries to our status quo so we would have something to protect in our twilight years.

The change journey that might lie ahead of us can't sidestep the fact that how well we love each other is the *most important item* on our report card.

Truth is, the stuff I thought we needed to change *from* was the stuff a former leader changed *to* a few decades before—and it worked back then. So today, when change is clearly needed, it makes sense that some put their hope in efforts that have a track record of success, even if we think these ideas are obviously outdated.

Maybe it's my age (I continue to insist that 60 still counts as mid 50s), but I've seen enough new ideas fail at becoming good ideas that I can understand why some folks put more faith in what has worked than what might work. Now, I love change—especially when I get to choose it—but experience tells me that latest doesn't always mean greatest; so I can justify a bit more patience with those who greet new ideas with a bit of skepticism, even when that new idea is mine. Someone's reluctance to leave the boat that's kept them afloat until they can be more sure that the engine in your new watercraft will start doesn't make them an old fogey. They just don't want to drown.

And by the way, the fourth item on our list is a reminder that *we didn't get where we are by ourselves.* In most cases, my congregation had been taught to trust in what they trusted. Some groups didn't trust at all for a similar reason: the one occupying my chair back then hadn't proven to be trustworthy. While we'll elaborate on this a bit more later, it bears mentioning that most pastors are leading journeys they didn't start. And we shouldn't use those struggles to justify criticism of the twelve photos on your wall, because we're all sowing seeds that someone else will likely harvest someday. But in this moment right now, the status quo we seem to be holding onto has been *our* way, *our* treasure, and *our* hope. We didn't get here without help. Someone taught us to believe in it the same way that you are trying to teach us to trust your plans today.

So yes, your change idea seems to imply that the last guy got something wrong. Yes, it feels a bit like we have to admit failure before we can embrace the possible successes connected to what you want to do. We understand when you call our ideas "old ways," but it hurts when you call them "wrong ways," because we were just giving our best to the last slate of someone's new ideas. "Status quo" may not be the best label for what we're clinging to. We want our church to be effective, to connect with our community, to see young people in our pews again. We've just been taught to trust in some patterns that may seem outdated to you, and we'll welcome your new ideas if you treat our old ones with a bit more respect.

People know that paradigms change. Today, your congregation may still be doing ministry according to the successful models of yesteryear, but that's the point—they *were* successful. Ridiculing their current ineffectiveness or assuming your people have settled for that ineffectiveness does little to encourage them to trust you or to embrace your new approaches.

Instead, see their passion and trust it.

There are certain moments I'll never forget from those first months in that aging Wichita church. There was the night a deacon dominated our monthly meeting with his passionate plea for our ministry to high school students. Though he was only a few years from retirement, his life as a schoolteacher had him weeping over the brokenness he saw every day in those letter-jacket-laced hallways. Our current efforts weren't enough—they never could be. These weren't imaginary mermaids just off our starboard bow. They were young lives at risk, and this man's front-row seat for their daily parade was more than he could contain.

Then, there was the 92-year-old guy who was convinced that God would let him live to see three hundred people worshipping at our church again.

Given that half his heart was non-functioning and doctors had considered his existence day-to-day for several years, it was hard not to be moved by his faith. The old guy was right. In fact, the doctors had to wait five more years to sign his death certificate, and by then, he'd seen the church reach the largest attendance in its long history.

And there was the day that about thirty of those older saints sat amidst pie and coffee as I, their much younger pastor, explained some of the changes we were engaging in together. I asked them to dream of their church in thirty years, realizing that few if any of us, would live to see that day. One dear lady said, "Pastor, we've given our lives to this church. In thirty years, we'd want this place to be greater than ever!" Wrinkled fists were raised unanimously in determined agreement.

As I've traveled amidst numerous flocks of all sizes and struggles, these are the kind of sheep I typically find. They want a future, they want to see their church's potential achieved, but some have banged into enough frustrating thorn bushes that they've chosen the center of the flock for safety. They want the greener grass and they know that the grass is always greener in the places that they've never been. It's just that they don't know how to get there.

I loved the passion of my older saints. No, their subsequent actions didn't always reflect that determination. Yes, they sometimes preferred the familiar ways of the past. But unlike my inability to understand my granddaughter's hunger, I knew what these folks were really feeling. They wanted a future, a legacy beyond their moment. They just didn't always know how to engage a necessary path that they'd never walked.

Neither did their pastor, but we tried hard to love each other as we searched for it—together.

So pastor, let me suggest a few things as we draw this passion chapter to a close. First, listen to what your people want you to know. . . . It's highly possible that you and your people won't agree on the steps of change to be taken because you may not want the same things. You want to build a great church and they want you to be a great pastor, but if you work together, you'll increase the likelihood that you both can get what you want.

It's highly possible that you and your people won't agree on the steps of change to be taken because you may not want the same things . . . but if you work together, you'll increase the likelihood that you both can get what you want.

Please hear them say, "We really want the same thing you do, even if we want it for different reasons. We want to reach people, we want our church to grow, we want to make a difference, because that's why we started this church many years ago. We believe in the same Great Commission that you preach to us about. In fact, we believed in it before you were the one preaching it. Our church isn't just a reflection of your ministry success or leadership skill. It's a reflection of who we are too. You see, the people in this community are our neighbors, our employers and employees, our kids' school friends and their families—they're our lives. So we're deeply vested in the impact we can make, and we believe you're here to help us do that better every day."

Second, consider a few steps that can make your future change journeys smoother and more effective:

1) Listen to the passion of your people. They hear yours a lot. You might be surprised by a school-teaching deacon or a fella who's already started his tenth decade on the planet. Find settings in which you can be the listener. You may need to help your church friends scrape the dirt off of those dreams, but it will be worth every such effort. Remember, they may have been listening to you and your predecessors for so long that their own voices have become a bit raspy, but patiently break up that dirt again and value the sounds their hearts make.

2) Trust their hearts, even if their hands and feet seem to act differently at times. Don't assume occasional expressions of resistance to mean that they're against you or that they just want the comfort of what they've known. They want more . . . they really do, and they love your efforts to help them reach for it.

3) Don't think your sheep are ignorant. They're really not. They may not have attended your seminary or mastered the subjects you've studied, but they're smart like you. And they know what they want, even if their ways of getting there aren't currently working. Respect the sheep, learn to love them, and together you can find the path forward.

4) Don't forget to feed them. If you can't lead them to green grass, making your flock larger won't be a good idea. So give yourself to their best and you'll be better equipped to provide what future sheep need, too. Plus, if you feed them well, the ones you have will soon be strong enough to help you when the new sheep arrive.

5) Finally, remember that under that shepherd's garb, you're really a sheep too. And the more you journey with this particular flock, the more you'll discover that you need them as much as they need you. You need their love and you'll thrive with their respect. But you gain these treasures only as you give them first.

Your people don't need you to be perfect. You don't have to be right every time. You're their shepherd, and they just want to trust your voice. So trust their passion.

CHAPTER TWO

PATIENCE . . .

Few things in life actually move at the speed
at which we want them to move.

Most of us would speed up traffic, unless you're that little old man in the farm truck who's raising his bony fist at anyone crazy enough to drive more than 45 miles per hour. Generally, we would like for meetings to move more quickly through their agendas, and some of us would like our spouses to do their hair more quickly when we're headed out to dinner—though we have only verbalized such thoughts once.

But we don't live every moment with both feet on the accelerator. Some moments find us wishing life came with brakes. So we stand at the bus stop on our child's first day of kindergarten, heartbroken that we've arrived at this occasion so soon. We plead with the math teacher to "slow down" when our algebraic questions are multiplying faster than our undivided attention can manage. And most of us have tried to slow the clock on our last day at the lake, our last goodbye at the airport, or just about any other "last" that we'd like more of.

Truth be told, few of us are pleased with the way time ticks on its predetermined cruise control. So we live each day begging our children to slow down and our parents to hurry up. We even find ourselves wanting to mess with God's speed. Every one of us at church has asked Him to move more quickly when unanswered prayers are on the line, or when blessings feel long overdue.

But pastor, we need you to move more slowly. When the issue is change and the victim is church, the people generally need their pastor to hear them when they say, "Give us time to trust you."

Time is an endangered resource. Though we get the same amount of it every day, we never have enough. Once my wife and some women from our church were chatting with a kindly, old gentleman as they walked along the coast of the Irish Sea. They were taking a break from the construction work of our mission trip—something I didn't think there was time for; but there really wasn't a good time to bring that up. Anyway, after an hour of chatting about the history of the quaint little village nearby, the beautiful flora and fauna of the overlooking hillside, and the possible identity of a distant boat, our ladies thanked the Irishman for taking the time to teach them so much about his homeland.

He replied, "O dearies, when God made time, He made plenty of it." That sounded so profound, and we subsequently found that phrase adorning many of the plaques, mugs, and key chains in Ireland's souvenir shops. It also explains why the Irish never achieved world domination. Everyone knows there's *never* enough time.

That's why a newly-minted pastor wants to get moving on his plans to fine-tune or completely rewire his church's ministry. He can see what they've been overlooking. He wants to prove his capacity to lead them toward greater effectiveness, and some of the needed steps seem quite obvious to him—rearrange the order of service, rip out some aging carpet, discontinue a few poorly-attended programs, launch a couple of new ideas. . . .

Slow down!

One of the lessons pastors tend to learn the hard way is that there's a definite gap between being the leader and earning the right to lead. The former can come as easily as being handed the ministry appointment and printing a box of business cards. There it is, in black and white: my name next to the church logo with the "p" word alongside for all to see! But if you think those business cards somehow give you the right to start using that carpet knife, well, you're probably going to cut off a few of your ministry fingers—and most of us have.

Earning the right to lead requires trust—a commodity that will be meted out slowly, at a pace that's affected not only by your actions but also, often, by the behavior of those who previously sat in your chair. In a healthy church that's enjoyed a relatively bump-less ride on the ministry roller coaster, the road to building trust can be clearly marked; but among those who've been jolted or even flown off the rails a few times, trust is often handed out with an eye-dropper.

In recent years, I've heard more than a few ultra-strong leaders proclaim their take-charge approach as the way to get things done. They've insisted that a pastor needs to make several changes in his first few weeks, while the people are still basking in the joy of finally having a new pastor. These are the days to establish a new world order. The first days are the best time to change things because the congregation will never be more ready for change than they are during the days in which they changed pastors—or so the thinking goes. Sadly, many who follow such advice are missing more than fingers. Some are just *missing*....

Earning the right to lead requires trust—a commodity that will be meted out slowly, at a pace that's affected not only by your actions but also, often, by the behavior of those who previously sat in your chair.

While there are a few remarkable leaders who can drive away the current congregation and have a new one here by next Sunday, most of us need a different strategy. If you're a new pastor who someday wants to be an old one, building trust is your better option.

A leader builds trust in one of four ways: relationship, success, unblemished integrity, and personal transformation. Let's consider each of these, discover how they build a foundation for change, and identify how much change each will allow a pastor to achieve before the ice beneath his feet begins to crack.

First, trust is built through *relationship*.

This used to be the pastor's wheelhouse. A new pastor would join his congregation, knowing that the best first step was to engage the people, get to know them and the extending branches of their families, and understand their worlds from an up-close perspective. Pastors once launched their ministries with plans for people rather than plans for change, believing they needed to walk in the former pastor's shoes for a while before being certain of any new steps.

Sunday sermons and Sunday dinners, wedding rehearsals and their subsequent receptions, graduation parties, hospital visits, kids' ballgames, family funerals—these and other moments like them prove to be the construction sites where a pastor's relationships are built. Pastor's influence in our lives is established by his presence in our lives. Experienced pastors understand that their preaching is a job requirement, but they really become "pastor" by their presence in the midst of life's major moments—especially its crises. Preach a great series on the Beatitudes and folks will appreciate you; but sit in the Intensive Care Unit and hold their hand as doctors remove dad's ventilator, and your role in their family changes forever.

And as that influence grows, trust grows as well. Through relationship, pastor has proven that he's one of us. We've come to know him as he has prioritized knowing us. So we attach ourselves and our family's spiritual futures to our pastor because we know him, we like him, and we trust him. Will we, then, let him direct changes in our church? Yes, at least to a point—the point that our relationship can withstand.

You see, when pastor has established healthy relationships with us, we come to believe that he understands us and our needs more fully. He does. So we are willing to trust his heart for us because he has proven that heart in our cemeteries and hospital wings. He's laughed at our jokes and eaten blueberry pie in our dining rooms. He has proven his commitment to us and we like him. Change? Go ahead, pastor, we trust you . . . to a point.

When your influence or leadership is built on relationship, we let you lead because we like you. But change too much or go too fast, and we start liking you less. "You may have done an amazing job with grandma's memorial service, but if you decide to discontinue my Sunday school class, we're back to square one!" This "zeroing out" of the love bank often catches pastor by surprise and inflicts some of his deepest hurts. He's caught off-guard when the family he's held together by the bailing wire of his late-night counseling efforts suddenly decides to leave the church. He doesn't understand how his long-time friend and fishing buddy withdraws his membership over last Sunday's song selection, or why the babies he's held and slipped candy to for a generation now want the Associate Pastor to replace him.

Yes, at times, we the people can be a bit fickle. We may allow our molehills to become mountains you can't climb, but there's something we need you to understand: in a journey of change, relationship is essential, but it will only take you so far. If we let you lead because we like you and then the changes you're making lead us to not like you anymore, you can see that your recent withdrawals from our love bank have overdrawn your account. So we close it.

Funny thing about relationships: though we won't let you make a lot of change with them, we won't let you make *any* change without them. Making changes at church without first building relationships is like trying to cash a check when you've never made a deposit—the bank teller's going to frown at you and shake her head until those horn-rimmed glasses fall from her ears.

Now, there are two modern realities that work against a pastor's priority of making relationships. The first of these is the increasing size of today's churches. A half-century ago, a pastor would typically arrive on scene and be welcomed by eighty to one hundred people who were ready to launch life's journey together. Today, that average has almost doubled, and there are many places where the assembled well-wishers could fill the local high school's gymnasium . . . twice. To build relationships with hundreds would be overwhelming. Keeping this size of a crowd happy requires a politician, not a pastor.

In the larger church, people soon figure out that a close relationship with their pastor isn't realistic. So we don't expect him to officiate the kids' wedding or show up at the clinic to pray before each colonoscopy. Instead, we like our pastor because he seems *likeable*—from a distance. We know him (or at least, we think we do) because of what he shows us in the pulpit. He's kind because he seems kind. He's smart because he sounds smart. He cares about us—you can tell by the way he crafts each week's benediction—but we really don't know him. We may, however, know some people who know him, and they say good things. In many larger churches, relationship isn't a realistic means for building trust. Pastors of congregations like these may have to look to one of the other options we'll consider in a moment.

The second reality is our principal subject in this chapter—time. Building relationships takes time. There really are no shortcuts. It's this requirement that causes many pastors to grow impatient. They're attending conferences where the latest idea looks like the perfect solution to an aspect of congregational weakness, but the concept of having to wait months or even years to try it out isn't appealing.

When I first became pastor of our congregation in Wichita, a fellow pastor told me that I wouldn't *really* be the pastor for the first five years I held the title. That's about how long it takes to build the relationships necessary to lead. He ruined my evening—several of them, in fact. I decided right there not to like that fellow pastor, and it had nothing to do with the fact that his congregation was six times larger than mine!

But he was right.

Relationship building is time-consuming work. And pastors—especially those leading congregations of 400 or less—have no choice but to make that investment. You simply cannot lead change until you have proven your love and care for the people, and that requires you to live life with them before launching everyone forward onto new avenues.

> Relationship building is time-consuming work. And pastors—especially those leading congregations of 400 or less—have no choice but to make that investment.

But this doesn't mean that you can't achieve change until you've entered year six. Change can be achieved more rapidly if you work effectively with those in the church who currently possess the influence you haven't had time to build. Often, those sitting around the deacon table or others on your leadership team have put in the time to prove their care for the congregation. If you can respect and value these friends and learn to trust their sense of judgment and timing, you can make earlier progress towards the future—steps you could never successfully take on your own.

Still, even with the help of these friends, you need to be prepared to spend some time before your congregation trusts you enough to let you determine their direction. Sheep follow their shepherd's voice, and it takes a little while for that voice to become familiar—time spent bringing us to green grass and extricating us from life's thorn bushes. We want you to lead us, but we need to be sure that you really *know* us before we can be sure that you know what's best.

The second way a leader builds trust is through *success*. Here, people begin to trust their pastor because he is achieving the church's goals. When great things are happening, we decide that he must know what he's doing, because look at the results we're seeing—Sunday attendance is up, the church's finances are strong, we're meeting our missions goals, people are committing their lives to Christ, and whatever other goals the church has identified are actually getting done. People love feeling like winners, and if the pastor is winning, well, he must be doing a good job!

Now first, we all know that no pastor deserves full credit for the victories a local church might celebrate. His efforts may be a part of the whole picture, but first applause is rightly aimed at God Himself. He's the one who's doing the real heavy lifting. Beyond that truth, we all know that it takes a team. Pastor might be doing all the preaching, but he's not doing all the inviting, all the giving, all the serving, all the praying, and all the other stuff we're currently celebrating. Still, if we stare at him when the church is struggling, it only makes sense to glance his way on the good days, too.

It's hard to argue with success—especially if we haven't succeeded for a while. Pastors who step in to lead plateaued or declining churches find that resistance melts away quickly if there's an influx of new people filling the pews or the altars. Those who argue for the status quo find the argument more difficult if what they oppose actually seems to be working. Of course, there are usually valid reasons for those past struggles, so suddenly finding a winning approach isn't as easy as writing about its possibility. Success, in the limited circumstances of the congregation, can cause us to feel like you know what we didn't—and that's something most of us will admit to if it means we can have a better day. You see, it's the *promise* of that better day that's not convincing—especially when few of us can remember the last time we lived in such blessing. The *reality* of such a better day sends an entirely different message.

Now what "works" is an awkward proposition for a local church's efforts. We can't afford the arrogance that puts too much confidence in methods or any other pride-feeder that has us thinking we've got this church thing figured out. But new ideas frequently spark new life; and if that life can be sustained and even expanded, well, spread the word! We've got a pastor who "knows what he's doing."

Trust that stems from success is quite different from the trust that relationship brings. In relationship-producing trust, the pastor earns my respect and confidence because I feel connected to him and the mission by which he lives. Conversely, in trust that's created by his perceived success, the sense of sharing in his efforts isn't always a factor. So *we* may trust pastor, but I'm not sure that *I* do. No, I'm not looking at him suspiciously or harboring negative attitudes that others don't possess. I'm not being negative at all. It's just that I may not feel like we're succeeding together. "He knows what he's doing, so let's listen to him" is a great deal different than, "He's proven that he loves us, so let's help him achieve the goals he believes are right for us."

Success-generated trust is often the necessary path for a pastor in a larger congregation. As we have said, the larger church doesn't allow for hundreds of relationships to sprout between people and pastor. Instead, these settings require that a pastor prove himself if he's going to make significant changes, and such proving can only be accomplished through measurable success. That's why pastors in larger churches may attempt change more quickly. They need to show the validity of their ideas and their direction in order to gain people's confidence. But even in the large church, moving too quickly—before we feel like we know our new leader—can prove catastrophic. For now, let's just say that the faster you try to implement change, the more critical it becomes to make the right moves.

Change initiatives at church will always be evaluated against some measure of success. In Old Testament times, prophets had to be on target every time if the people were to conclude that God was the voice behind their messages. Pastors don't have to meet such a perfect standard. Their ideas don't have to succeed every time, but perceived failure today will affect how much we trust your next idea tomorrow. Add in a history of failure from someone else's previous efforts, and you have a congregation that may keep you from trying new steps, regardless of the success they're convinced that you could bring.

While success can bring trust, there are some pitfalls. First, not everyone uses the same scorecard. Higher numbers of people attending services may cause some to rejoice, but others might see the larger crowd as intimidating or stealing from the attention they crave for themselves. More people signing up for the worship team seems like a good thing, but those already on the team may not rejoice that they're now needed a little less often. When people want to resist change, they may deny *any* suggestion of success, ignoring good signs while magnifying less critical areas of continued struggle. You may hear, "Sure, Sunday attendance is up this month, but that won't last long. Besides, there's been no growth in our midweek service, so these new people aren't really the committed kind."

To tackle the scorecard issue, you need to establish one. If people get to choose their own idea of success, those who resist change will focus on areas that make any new efforts seem unsuccessful. But don't play the game the other way and simply highlight the areas that make your ideas look good. There's more to a church's forward movement than nickels and noses, as important as such measures might be. Let your vision for change define your scorecard in the healthiest way possible, and then you can start celebrating the right wins.

The second challenge with trust that's achieved through success is what can happen to that trust when the success slows down. Momentum can be a wonderful thing, but once it slows, getting progress started again can be difficult. If we use success to convince people that pastor knows what he's doing, then a lack of success can send the opposite message. For this reason, a success path to trust can be exhausting for the leader. When next week must top this week in order to maintain congregational confidence, unhealthy expectations will form. Congregational life has some natural ups and downs. If too much confidence depends on our weekly successes, the challenge of continually-increasing victories will soon become unrealistic.

A third means for building trust is to act with *integrity*. When people see that a leader will always do what is right, they begin to trust that leader with what is right for them. Someone has defined integrity as "what you do when no one is looking." It's the idea of what you're really like when you're not performing for others. That presents an interesting opportunity for pastors, since they are almost always "on." Their 24-7 life as a shepherd seldom lets them take the pastor hat off.

A pastor can establish his public persona through wise words, penetrating insights, and the understanding demeanor with which he preaches. People say, "He's just a really good guy." He shows up when we're in crisis. He speaks kind words at our grandmother's funeral. He stands at the church door, always smiling, always listening, always affirming. He speaks knowledgeably about the godly husband when he teaches on marriage, and more than a few women wish their own husband was more like him. *He's a great guy!*

When people see that a leader will always do what is right, they begin to trust that leader with what is right for them.

But hold up the private places of his life, and the photos may not always match. If people see him yell at his children, become frustrated with his wife, or offer a small fib or two when negotiating a good price with a salesman, the photo of the pastor they *think* they know gets a bit smudged—and trust becomes a bit damaged.

I remember attending a conference in which an elderly leader held us spellbound for more than an hour as he unfolded the challenges of reaching the next generation. He spoke of younger people with such passion and potential. He called for great steps to be taken to rally his older peers toward a bright and technologically-driven future. I remember thinking, "That's the kind of leader anyone would want to follow. The people who work in his organization have to be excited to have such a leader."

Then, I went to the hotel restaurant for a late dinner. There, at a corner table, sat the amazing leader, hidden behind the tall menu he was perusing. I chose a booth not too far away so the waitress wouldn't have to walk too far to serve us. The speaker and I were the only customers in the restaurant at that late hour. Soon, I was hiding behind my own menu.

When our food was delivered—his before mine, since he had had a head start on the menu—the speaker's order was apparently assembled incorrectly. The vegetable was wrong, promised sauces were missing, and there was no butter for his bread. I knew each of these errors because he screamed them at the poor girl who had brought his plate. I sat stunned as he berated her for someone else's negligence. I couldn't believe that the man who had seemed so wise, so kind, and so in touch with today's young people two hours earlier could abuse one such young person only a stone's throw from the podium where he was so remarkable. Even as I write this, I realize that I remember his behavior in the restaurant, but can't recall any of the incredible content of his evening message. I've apparently lost the notes I took, too.

When the message matches the man (or woman), trust grows. A pastor who cuts corners, takes advantage of others, or seeks things for himself undermines such growth. But one who proves to be real—who acts honestly in every transaction, who treats people up close with his same "pulpit-kindness," and who insists on doing what is right even when that truth proves costly—that's the pastor who will gain our trust.

If our pastor can be trusted in the little things, we will more quickly trust him with the big things. And if he turns out to be that other guy, we may never learn to trust him at all. Now, no pastor is perfect, and most people try hard to provide their pastor with a little grace to cover the occasional difficult moment. But the spotlight remains on at all times—even when you think you're eating alone in a hotel restaurant.

The final means by which trust can be achieved is *personal transformation*. Here, we have decided to trust our pastor because of the impact his ministry has had on our lives. In the work of making disciples, those who shape lives establish a powerful influence on the lives they have shaped. So we say, "Pastor, your efforts have changed our lives. Now we trust you to change our church."

Personal transformation builds the most powerful form of trust possible in a ministry relationship. You can see such impact modeled in the relationships Jesus shared with His disciples. After a few years of almost-daily interaction with Jesus' teaching and miraculous moments, the disciples were ready to be world-changers on His behalf. When His work in their lives was punctuated by His resurrection—a moment that made their own deaths a lot less threatening—they circled the globe with His message, enduring death threats towards themselves and standing firm when those threats became reality. He had changed their lives, so now they trusted Him completely.

Of course, personal transformation is no overnight achievement. In fact, of the four methods of building trust, this one likely takes the most time. But it's also the reason most of us became pastors anyway: we want to make a difference, and we hope to do it in the lives of people. To some degree, personal transformation can be understood as a combination of the relationship and success approaches. It begins with a genuine commitment to the existing congregation—to grow them, serve them, and teach them to serve others. As that priority becomes clearer, the people are strengthened to aid our pursuit of the church's measures of success. When we feel loved and understood, we will roll up our sleeves with you—and that's often where we find the life change we've long desired for ourselves.

If you want to grow a church without growing its people, you'll be found out soon enough. Selfish success stories seldom endure in the local church. Frankly, it's hard to imagine God Himself getting on board with such an agenda or allowing one of his local families to suffer one for very long. Congregations are rarely enthused about building a name for their pastor, especially if they get very little out of the bargain themselves. I think we can assume that God is on their side on that one. Instead, a pastor's genuine desire to see his people discover life as it's meant to be lived keeps the focus where it rightly belongs.

Regardless of the numbers in the sanctuary, we need to sense your heart for us, and the hope you have for what we can become.

While personal transformation will usually prove to be the most powerful means of building trust, it can also be the most difficult to measure. Pastor's presence alongside my hospital bed can prove he loves me, and there are metrics we can use to identify our church's successes, but how do I know when personal transformation is occurring? What measuring stick can we use to determine real progress, and how can a pastor reach higher on that stick?

The answer is usually told in the stories we're living.

Pastor, if you're going to have this kind of impact on our lives, we need to see your passion for the lives we currently have. Regardless of the numbers in the sanctuary, we need to sense your heart for us, and the hope you have for what we can become. Some of us stopped dreaming a while ago, and our family members haven't mentioned our potential in quite some time. When you teach and preach in a way that says you believe in us and want to walk with us into our futures, we know you didn't come to our church just to reach other people. You want to reach *us*, too.

I love visiting Mt. Rushmore—that chiseled collection of granite presidential heads one can find amidst South Dakota's Black Hills. As a huge Abe Lincoln fan, I can spend hours at any site where he is in focus. Add Washington, Jefferson, and Teddy Roosevelt, and you've more than tripled the attraction.

Why those four? Actually, Gutzon Borglum, the original sculptor at Rushmore, rejected the first list of carving candidates suggested by the guy who dreamed of the monument in the first place. Lewis and Clark, Red Cloud, and Buffalo Bill surely impacted the west, but Borglum insisted on sculpting those who had made their mark on a wider scale. Good call. These four great men had transformed a nation. Washington, Jefferson, Lincoln, and Roosevelt had founded, expanded, and preserved this superpower and therefore symbolized its courage. As such, they are among the most trusted leaders in our nation's history.

Who would be on Mt. Rushmore if it were *your* life we were celebrating? For me, the list is easy—my dad, my immigrant grandfather, my first pastor, and his young adult son. I won't fill the pages it would require to explain how each of these men have transformed my life, but I can think of no one whose head should be carved on my life's mountain ahead of theirs.

Now, seeing family members on that list shouldn't be too surprising, but including my pastor and his son seem significant to this context. Actually, Pastor Howard held that title in my life for twenty-six years, and his ministry has certainly impacted every other year since. He put my growth, and the life advancement of dozens of others, ahead of any church growth agenda he may have harbored. His son lived the same way, leading me to my initial faith decision and becoming a valued mentor in my teen years. They, along with my dad and grandfather, shaped my life in ways I can't fully describe. Rushmore's reserved for folks like that.

Pastor, we can tell when that's who you want to be for us. You know our names, remember chunks of our important stories, and help us target a destination for our futures. So you bring the passion and we'll bring our very lives—the stories such a merger will write could prove to be the best future our church can find. You may want to change the way we do church, but your greater goal is to change us more into what we really want to be. Frankly, we'll be glad for you to change both.

These are the paths to influence—relationship, success, integrity, and personal transformation. Individually, they each may fall short or be beyond your ability to clearly measure, but a combined effort will make a major difference. I'd suggest you target all four so you can accelerate our trust and maximize your own ministry effectiveness. But the point is that these are the paths—the ONLY paths—to gaining our trust.

So pastor, listen carefully to what your people want you to know—give us time to trust you. Sadly, George Barna tells us that the average tenure of a pastor has declined to four years, even though studies consistently show that pastors experience their most productive and influential ministry in years five through fourteen of their pastorate. Thom Rainer's survey shows even shorter ministry spans—3.6 years on average—while a survey of effective pastors reveals an average of 11.2 to 21.6 years.

What's your hurry?

Pastor, please understand that time is your friend. When you take the time to build trust, you are also investing in your ultimate effectiveness. Rome wasn't built in a day, and churches can seldom be changed in a week. The shepherd-sheep connection is designed for the long haul. You tread on life's most critical issues, and we turn to you in its most difficult challenges. That kind of relationship demands more than just an hour each week. It calls for both pastor and people to bring our entire selves to the table.

In this same vein, there's one more truth your people really need you to understand: *We want to trust you.*

Never forget that people come to church by choice. While there may be a few teenagers attending against their wills, everyone else walked through your stained-glass entry voluntarily. And while they engage their faith with differing degrees of intensity, the point is that they need you and want you and have hopes for your connection with them that may not be much different than your own goals. You're the shepherd, and the sheep really want to follow after you.

Yes, your people may not always act consistently with that image. But don't assume their worst moments are the best reflection of who they are. You see, some pastors misread the resistance they face. In places where hurt has been more common than hope, we shouldn't be surprised at the bark and bite we must overcome. Trust is a fragile commodity. When it's been damaged, rebuilding it is never an exact science, no matter who's doing the building.

Everyone has a story. And those who seem to see life through the darkest glasses almost always prove to have the blackest journeys. Betrayal and disappointment—both real and imagined—carve deep crevices in one's spirit, ravines you can't fill with a few Sunday handshakes and a complimentary church coffee mug. So give hurting people time for the real story to slowly emerge. If you do, a day of healing might one day be discovered.

Simply put, trust, no matter how desperately needed and longed for, will always measure its progress in calendar pages.

CHAPTER THREE

PAST . . .

They're really good people.

He'd been staring at me all morning with an expression unlike any in the room. I'd been teaching for over an hour. A hundred local church leaders and their pastors were gathered around tables, preparing to dive into a year-long journey of discovery and discussion. Our goal? Find the future for the dozen or so congregations represented in the room.

Things at his table didn't look too promising. His pastor looked like a good guy. He'd been at the church for a couple of years now and seemed determined to slow the church's decade of steady decline. I wanted to believe he could. This pastor appeared enthusiastic, and his wife seemed to genuinely enjoy the people at their table. Better days were ahead, I was sure . . . except for the look on this one guy's face.

This is what I do. I work with churches, trying to help them navigate a climb to greater effectiveness or turn a downward spiral in a new, more promising direction. Some days, I sit with leaders from one congregation. Other days, the door's been opened to multiple congregations, and I try to aid the unique discovery of purpose and direction occurring at each of the room's round tables. This was one of those days.

But he wasn't buying it. Every other face showed signs of genuine engagement. These people had come to learn. Motivational speeches aren't usually needed when folks give up an entire Saturday to help their pastor find answers. Each participant had been chosen for this assignment. Pastor needed their faith, their hope, and their ability to dream with him. It's usually a fun room. This one man wasn't having fun. His face didn't fit with the others. They smiled and nodded and jotted notes vigorously. He pushed his chair back further from the table, folded his arms, and glared at me as though he'd accepted a mission to prove me wrong at every turn. I could read his thoughts (not really). I could anticipate his complaints (I'd heard them before). I could quote his list of reasons why nothing I suggested would ever work at his church (I figured he was the reason).

We made it to the lunch break without him derailing my confidence. I wanted to embrace the affirmation the others in the room extended as I grabbed a sandwich and a plate full of chips, but he was too close. By the time I reached the drink table, he had me cornered and asked if he could sit with me.

Now, I'm a pastor—at least, I had been one for quite a while. Most of us know when we're about to receive someone's well-meaning correction. You've heard it too—the auditorium was too cold on Sunday or the sermon was too long, or in that one announcement we failed to mention the part that everyone really needed to know. Such moments are meant to help us, to make us aware of what people are saying, all the while being sure that the messenger means no ill intent. So I slid my tray in front of a couple of empty chairs and motioned for my new friend to join me. I quickly took a bite of my sandwich, believing that the chewing motion would hide any other reactions my face might have toward his rebuke. But then something else happened, and I wasn't as prepared as I'd thought for what the next few moments would bring.

He wept. His shoulders began to vibrate and he fought hard to muffle the sobs that wanted to burst forth. "You don't understand," he whispered, trying to keep his overwhelming emotion from drawing the attention of the room. "You don't understand ... I can't see a future ... we can't have a future for our church when we're all afraid to face the past."

Suddenly, my food didn't taste so good. I tried to swallow quickly, anxious to console him, wanting to trade in my suspicions for a much-needed dose of compassion. Pastor had seen the tears and slid into the seat next to me. "What is it, Bill?" he asked in such a soft voice that Bill and I could see his concern. In an instant, I went from the center of a conversation to its bystander, and I knew that I needed to do just that.

"Pastor, you don't know all that's happened. You don't know about the Jenkins and the Simpsons, and the thing with the Walkers." There was no reaction. The names didn't seem to register in the pastor's expression. "How can we talk of vision and a future when we can't deal with all the hurt of the past?"

Good question, Bill.

After a brief conversation and the pastor's pledge to engage whatever hurt Bill and his other tablemates might be carrying, our afternoon resumed. Bill wiped his eyes with a friend's oversized handkerchief and pulled his chair back up to the table, seemingly ready to participate now that he was sure his new pastor really cared enough to face the ugliness that had been a part of where they'd been. Over the next few months, Bill was as pleasant and engaging as anyone in the room. Apparently, he was finding reasons to reach for the future again.

But his question underscores something your people want you to know before you lead them in change, Pastor: "We'll go where you go if you'll come where we are."

In the first chapter, we discussed how pastor and people are apt to get off to a challenging start when their goals for the relationship differ. Remember, he wants to build a great church and they just want a great pastor. Well, one of the reasons for that disconnect is the simple fact that, Pastor, you've stepped into the middle of a story.

Have you ever tuned into a movie an hour in? Ever tried reading a book by starting in Chapter Six? Do you know what it feels like to walk up to a group of friends who are fully engrossed in a story one of them has been telling for the last ten minutes?

Confusing, isn't it?

You really don't know what's going on or what has already occurred. How can you possibly guess what might or should happen next? Thanks to modern technology, some people won't even watch an episode of a popular television show until they can go back three seasons and start at the beginning. It's the backstory we need if we're going to understand the story ahead. So how do we think we can lead a church forward without catching up on the episodes that have shaped the current plot? Things didn't start when our current pastor walked in the door, and pretending that they did isn't fooling anyone.

Now, if you're a church planter, the founding pastor of your congregation, or that rare breed that ends up pastoring the church you grew up in, then you know much, if not all, of the road that's been previously traversed. You've been there and done that, and you should have a handle on how yesterday might be impacting today. In fact, you could skip to the next chapter of this book, but I think we'll still cover some ground in this one that you'll find helpful.

Things didn't start when our current pastor walked in the door, and pretending that they did isn't fooling anyone.

For the rest of us, there's a history lesson ahead.

Frankly, one of the surprises I find at many of these group gatherings reveals itself when I ask each group about the age of their church. They know, but I am amazed at how often the pastor doesn't. Now, pastors are typically ready with the answers to most of my questions, but on this one they quickly glance at the older fella on their left to find out. That's a smart thing to do when you don't know. I've had a few pastors venture a guess only to miss the correct response by more than a decade. That's awkward.

The night my wife and I were elected to serve as lead pastors at Maranatha Worship Center in Wichita, the deacons sent us home with two books. The first was a small but beautifully bound copy of the church's constitution and bylaws. No staples or plastic spiral combs for these folks. When a congregation pays to publish the bylaws with such quality, you can quickly imagine some of the reasons this document has become so important over the years.

The second book was larger—a hardback history of the nearly eight decades this congregation had lived together. Black and white photos and the detailed descriptions provided by the church's official historian proved that every moment of their journey mattered, even now. The book had been assembled for their 75th anniversary celebration a few years earlier. Though I knew that such effort to tell a church's story usually means that yesterday looks more appealing than today or tomorrow, I was pleased to have access to such a valuable publication.

But I have to be honest: I didn't read it as attentively as I should have. The weeks prior to moving my family to our new home and new city were filled with plans. I was busy crafting vision statements and listing ministry priorities. I was writing a core discipleship class and thinking about the process we would use for equipping new believers. There were books to read, but they were the practical strategies that some of the most successful pastors had poured into notebooks and video discussions. If podcasts weren't still eight years from invention, I would have listened to them, too. What had happened at this church didn't seem nearly as important to me as what was about to occur—at least, this is what I must have been thinking. So when I arrived at my new office and unpacked my library, I placed that history book on my coffee table—which, by the way, is the right place for a coffee table book.

They say that those who don't learn from history are destined to repeat it. I'm not sure that's true in every situation. What I do believe is that, if you don't learn your church's history, you will run smack into it. And it'll likely hit you hard. It's tragic to learn things the hard way when an easier path is sitting on your coffee table.

Here's what you can learn ... *yours isn't our first vision.*

There's something exciting about a fresh start with a new pastor. You can tell as you watch the Sunday attendance swell a bit on that first weekend. Even some of those who had drifted away in recent months stop by again—people come to see. What are they looking for? That's a bit hard to pinpoint. Some may have felt rejection from a previous leader and now look to see if there's any single-Sunday evidence that the new regime will be different. Some miss their old friends and see leadership change as an opportunity to reenter without having to answer a lot of questions. Some may be wondering who else left after they did, since they figured theirs would be the first of many departures.

But most come to see what the new day will look like. They come to hear the new priorities that will be undertaken. They come to feel the direction of an altered journey to determine if the church will now choose a destination they'd like to find. In a word, they come for the vision.

Vision is a difficult word. It suffers from overuse, to the point that any clear sense of its intended meaning has been obscured by the dozen or so alternative meanings it's been known to carry. Vision can mean many things to many people, much like the idea of "love" and the specific manifestations of "flu." You just can't use such words without explaining what you really mean.

In this instance, vision's definition is in the eye of the beholder. What did that slightly-enlarged crowd come looking for? What were they hoping to hear or to settle in their minds by darkening the door on our new pastor's first Sunday? And what was it they apparently didn't hear or didn't like, since their Sunday attendance didn't reproduce itself? In such moments, vision means new direction and destination, along with the strategies that will get us there. While that's more than the word really should mean, a pastor's sense of vision must produce it all. He must tell us where we are going, why we are going there, and how we will most likely get there. That's what Moses brought down from the mountain, and that's what we're looking for from the new Moses who just moved his family into our tiny parsonage. What's God telling us to do, how is He telling us to do it, and what will things look like when we've done it?

That's a lot of pressure on poor Moses, especially if he hasn't been up the mountain yet.

Truth is, a new pastor can't and shouldn't have all those answers on his first Sunday. He just joined our carpool; and even if we decide to let him drive that first day, the only places he knows how to find are the places he's already been. He could try to superimpose the road map of his last church on us, but that's probably not a journey that fits in the new place. So how can he know where we're going or start to know how to get there?

Vision is hard, and how to find it deserves its own book; but what we really need pastor to know is that we've been down this road before—*more than once.*

As I already mentioned, I was pastor number thirteen. From everything I could tell, those other twelve guys were pretty remarkable. Though many had died before I started to live, some of the names were quite familiar. There was the prominent missionary whose amazing stories among cannibals in Liberia were the stuff of legends. Little wonder that the great missionaries to emerge from this historic congregation were launched during the late 1920s era, when his vision ruled the roost. There were the denominational leaders, a few of whom had spent time amidst this congregation on their way to bigger things. The footprints of their excellence were still discernable in the hallway carpet and in the hearts of those they once led. There was the guy whose evangelistic zeal had guided the days of the church's greatest attendance. Busses in the 1960s had brought dozens of children and parents to the door—a strategy that swelled the black and white sanctuary photos of those days until it seemed the building would hold no more (I finally got around to reading that history book).

And there was my predecessor, the brave saint who'd led the church's aggressive and under-resourced move to the suburbs. It wasn't easy to abandon the deteriorating building that his vision had inherited for the temporary comforts of a shopping mall until a new campus was ready. It wasn't easy enduring the financial failings of a general contractor that left much of the finishing work to his aging congregation. It wasn't easy, but he did it—by vision.

Unfortunately, as is often the case, twelve pastors meant twelve visions. And after you've rambled in the wilderness chasing after that many different oases, it's hard not to lose your own way. Just like in your church, pastor. Once the people have been led to pursue a few different visions, their anticipation of the next one wanes a bit. If the last couple of chases have done little to quench their desperate thirst, don't be shocked if your enthusiasm for a new journey is met with a bit of barely-veiled ambivalence. We've been here before.

Now, that doesn't mean we don't want to go with you or that we've all purchased subscriptions to "Better Homes and Deserts," and want to plant radishes in the sand. We want the new day you hope to bring; it's just that we've been down a few roads already. That's why those folks didn't come back after they dipped their toes in the water on your first weekend. We want vision, we need vision—but after we've lived through several visions, vision just doesn't rev our engines like it used to.

You've probably heard about the frog that once battled the limits of the jar that contained him. In his early days, he jumped a lot, banging his somewhat slimy green head on the underside of the lid until repeated bouts of dizziness taught him a new way. Now, he doesn't jump as often, and certainly not as high—so go ahead and use that lid on a jelly jar (just wash it first).

Frankly, church can be a place where we talk a great deal about what we're going to do and why we should do it, but it's not always a great place for *doing it*. Motivation without strategy has doomed many a vision, and left us with a keen awareness of the gap between where we are and where we could be. Add thoughts of God and His purposes to this mix, and "could be" starts feeling like "should be." Pastor, don't think we're not interested in the new day you dream of. We truly are. But yours isn't our first lap on the vision track, and some of us still have sore muscles from the last time we tried to sprint. We're a bit more cautious now, and we might need some pre-race stretching.

Remember my friend Bill? He was the fella struggling to see a future for his church because the past was demanding attention. Like a driver with an 18-wheeler bearing down on him, he was struggling to give any attention to the windshield. Sometimes, the monsters in the rearview mirror really are closer than they appear to be. Bill's story is sadly far more common than most of us realize. When you become the pastor of a local congregation, there are many stories you don't know and haven't been a part of—and a lot of them aren't good ones. In fact, people don't talk about them, and if they do, they only whisper.

To effectively lead many established churches into the future, a pastor has to have a grasp of the past. You see, the past has shaped the present and it has molded some of its participants, too. Over the years, several people have told me that I tend to walk too quickly. For whatever reason, my approach to where I'm going occurs at a pace that's uncomfortable for many of those who walk with me. I've been known to escape the sight of those following me through airports or traipsing toward the work site on a church mission trip. "Can we slow down a bit?" they ask politely, though I'm guessing they may be mumbling other things.

> To effectively lead many established churches into the future, a pastor has to have a grasp of the past.

I admit that I walk fast. The "too fast" part is the opinion of others. And chief among them is my wife, who frequently reminds me that we're not in the hurry my legs seem to believe we're in. Now, my wife is an aggressive high-achiever who, like me, packs more into her calendar than some find realistic. She's not slow by any definition. My guess is that the difference in our paces relates to leg length and one other major factor—shoes.

I'm no expert on women's shoes, and I tread cautiously here so as to avoid losing what could be more than half of my readers. But it seems to me that, in women's shoes, there's often an inverse relationship between attractiveness and functionality. When Nancy Sinatra originally sang, "These Boots Are Made For Walkin'," she probably had a specific set of footwear in mind. So did Jessica Simpson when she revived and recorded the same tune, though I'm guessing that her closet offers a variety to choose from. The song suggests that each of these musical women had other options in their closets, but they weren't made for "walkin'."

I've never worn women's shoes and have no plans to do so; but I'm convinced that, should I ever don a high heel, the speed of my gait would surely be affected. Simply put, if I walked in my wife's shoes, I wouldn't walk faster than she can.

The idea of walking "in someone else's shoes" implies understanding where they've been and what they're dealing with from an insider's perspective. It means exploring what we feel about the journeys we've faced and how those journeys may currently be killing our feet or even hurting our hearts. A leader who ignores the impact of where we've been will never understand us enough to effectively lead us in a new direction—no matter how wonderful the waters of your Promised Land might be for soaking our feet. You need to take a few steps in our shoes.

That's what we're asking you to do, Pastor.

A second fact many pastors will discover when they look into the congregational past is that *we've got our share of dysfunction.*

No congregational journey can be reviewed without discovering a fair number of detours, wrong turns, and family quarrels in the car. Welcome to humanity, the necessary risk God took when entrusting His eternal purposes to us. We tend to get things wrong on the road to getting them right.

One of the greatest ventures in human history begins unfolding in the Bible's book of Exodus. Moses, a slave baby raised in the palace, leads masses of oppressed Israelites to a land of freedom and plenty. It's a compelling story with every plot line the most creative screenwriters could possibly manufacture. That's why every movie ever filmed of those events gets the label "epic." It's an amazing story. But think about this story from a bird's-eye view. First, you have such an amazing vision—the Promised Land: a gift to people who'd spent more than four centuries in slavery. We've lived the American dream for a little more than two centuries. Imagine facing your greatest nightmare for twice that amount of time, only to have the horror melt into a hope like this one. Honestly, the idea was so appealing that even a bunch of Egyptians gave up their homes to follow those slaves into the desert.

Of course, this was God's journey. He proved He was along for their ride on numerous occasions. First, He extricated them from Pharaoh's grip with the help of ten horrific plagues, aiming them into the Egyptian neighborhoods with a precision that makes our smart bombs look like kindergarten projects. Then, He dropped a moving sidewalk into the middle of the Red Sea, creating an aquatic adventure not even Sea World can copy. Maybe they could, if anyone would have taken a few photos— but there wasn't time, as God Himself collapsed that body of water into a frenzy of waves that washed away the powerful army chasing them.

There was honey-soaked bread-like stuff on the ground. There was water from a rock, and quail that flew so low and so slowly that even the senior adults were catching them in their bare hands. I've hunted quail a few times and know firsthand what a miracle that would take. To say that God made the journey with them seems to be a colossal understatement. Don't forget the cloud. God put a puffy tour guide in the skies to show them when and where to move forward, and He even lit that fuzz ball up with fire at night so they'd be warm and confident of His direction, even while they were sleeping.

And Moses was a pretty good leader himself. The book of Hebrews lauds his humility, and it's clear that this former Egyptian prince had a heart for God that few can match. If you want to be a leader, it's hard to find a finer example to follow than Jochebed's boy.

Put that all together: you have amazing vision, God's power and presence punctuating the journey in "you-had-to-be-there" kind of ways, supernatural guidance so clear that even the most foolhardy could see which way to go, and a leader of leaders who easily falls among human history's *Top Ten Guys to Follow Anywhere.*

And *still*, there was dysfunction. People complained and wanted to go back to the land of slavery where they were now hated with immeasurable fury. Some of the leaders were prone to backbiting and jealousy. They even called God's spotless record of support into question when their enemies became bigger. Frankly, if there was ever a journey that should have danced all the way to the end, this was it. A real life musical in the making, and yet they hit an awful lot of sour chords.

Every journey has problems . . . yours will too. So, Pastor, as you look at where we've been, be gentle. Too many new leaders try to build their current credibility on the failures of the past. They vocalize the frustrations of the formerly frustrated, thinking that affirming their disagreement with former leaders somehow aids their own popularity. They point out the mistakes of the past, hoping people realize that, "had I been here," the path would have been straighter. So trashing the predecessor or ridiculing the past becomes the path to a weak leader's future.

He won't live to see it.

Every journey has problems . . . yours will too. So, Pastor, as you look at where we've been, be gentle.

If you criticize the day you didn't live and the road you didn't walk, you alienate those who did. Sure, there were mistakes along the way; but the last thing we need is for someone to remind us of that. Besides, that leader you're refuting cared about us, led us in circumstances you don't fully understand, and sought the same God for direction that we need *you* to talk to now. Don't ridicule the work that preceded your arrival. You won't earn our respect that way.

Change, on its own, can feel like a criticism of the past. A new way causes some to think you've decided that the old way was foolish. Don't add to these inaccurate perceptions with careless words and actions that seem to prove them true. The Apostle Paul wasn't afraid to confront unhealthy stuff when necessary, but even he told us to prove all things and do your dancing around the good stuff (somewhat paraphrased). If you want to lead our next step, affirm the steps we've already taken. You may be smarter than our last pastor, but if you insist on *acting like it*, some of us will feel compelled to prove otherwise. He was our friend first. Even if he made a mess of things and limped away in colossal failure, it's not fun to gloat over his grave. We need to build with rock, not mud.

So Pastor, we know you're anxious to get started on the future, but let us walk you through our past a bit. We need you to know a few things before we put this car in drive.

We need you to know that *you've missed a lot.*

We need you to know that *yours isn't our first vision.*

We need you to know that *getting this far hasn't been easy.*

We need you to *be gentle when discovering our failures.*

And we need you to *walk in our old shoes a bit before thinking we can run in your new ones.*

We're all a part of a larger story: a tale we hope will reach epic measurements, and your people want you to be everything your role requires. They'll even help you by doing their parts. Just don't think that this story started the day they added your name to their bulletin. It didn't, and there's a lot of stuff behind them that they'll keep carrying until you lovingly help them lay it down.

Here's what happens if you do: if you love them enough to listen to their stories and let them cry through the sad parts, they'll write new stories with you. They don't need you to fix them—at least not yet. They don't need you to run your highlighter over their failures—they know them too well. They simply need you to love them enough to know that you can learn from them too. And they'll teach you what a few forays into the tall weeds have taught them. You both need to know those things, because they *really* don't want to end up there again.

Bill turned out to be a really good guy. In fact, by the end of our journey together, he was ready to stand before his congregation and use his influence to fuel the new direction he and his team had discovered. Turns out that he's the kind of guy you'd love to have in your church. To say that he's a believer in his congregation's future today would be an understatement. I'm guessing there are several folks in that church reeling in shock to see Bill becoming such a catalyst for change. Last I saw, he was joyfully flailing his arms to fan that flame. It feels really good to see him so enthusiastic. Like most of us, he's a lot better looking when he smiles.

Funny thing, though: I keep running into Bill nearly everywhere I go. Actually, it's not Bill himself, but maybe a few of his cousins. In so many settings, I find people twisted into a tight ball that will only ever be unraveled when a wise and caring pastor takes the time to do what Bill's pastor did for him.

CHAPTER FOUR

PEOPLE . . .

Different church, different people. . . .

During my junior year, I proudly wore blue and gold as a member of my high school basketball team. We were the Cougars, a proud basketball powerhouse—at least among the other small Christian schools in our region. I jogged onto the court every game for the pre-game warm up, knowing I wouldn't get much other exercise that evening. That I was on the team at all was more a testimony to our school's size than my own basketball prowess. I was 5'7" tall with a jump shot my sister once blocked. But the school had purchased a dozen or so uniforms and bodies were needed to fill them, so I did. We had really cool uniforms.

Now, we had a good team, but you could say that we were even more impressive on paper. At one tournament, we discovered an error in the program that had somehow added one foot of height to five of us who sat on the bench. Our tallest player on the entire team was actually 5'11", but the program listed some of my fellow benchwarmers as 6'10", 6'8", 6'9", and 6'10". I was 6'7" tall that weekend, according to the document that six dozen or so fans paid $1 to read. I must admit it felt good, but no one would believe my insistence that my warmup pants were now too short.

Our coach insisted that the error in the program was typographical, but we assumed he was looking for a strategic advantage. You see, if opposing coaches saw that program, they would be scrambling to realign their strategies. After all, how do you prepare your team for the basketball challenges of facing such massive high school opponents? Like the Looney Tunes movie *Space Jam*, we were the Monstars to their Bugs Bunny. And unfortunately for Bugs, Michael Jordan was still in middle school.

But we weren't that team. Typos don't really make you tall.

I don't remember how that tournament turned out for me and my fellow Cougars. But I do know that, if my coach or anyone else expected us to be what the program suggested we were, it wasn't going to happen. I would have loved to be able to rebound as if I was a foot taller. I would have been thrilled to fly through the air, catch a pass, and dunk the ball with NBA-level authority. Seriously—that's the kind of thing I'd been dreaming about since preschool, but things hadn't worked out. All those hours hanging by my arms from my backyard swing set hadn't added one inch to my vertical expanse. I wasn't 6'7", and now that I've entered my sixties, I'm starting to think I never will be.

We can't be what we aren't. And Pastor, that's one of the things your people need you to understand about your effort to lead them in change: *we're not your last church or the church you've read about in church growth books.*

———————————————

In some church traditions, including the one I've called home my entire life, we have high expectations of our pastoral leaders. Not only do we expect them to be able perform all the necessary tasks of ministry—speaking, administrating, counseling, coordinating, fundraising, training, comforting, and befriending—we also expect it to be done while we joke that they only work one day a week.

We're not your last church or the church you've read about in church growth books.

Okay, maybe we know better than that; but one of the expectations we place on a pastor is to know the answer to just about every question, especially the one about direction and vision for our church. We can see that our church is in decline, or getting older, or not reaching new people, or reaching them but not turning them into active and supportive members, or whatever else might concern you about the direction of your church. Pastor, we need to do something—and you're expected to know what that is!

As I said, we have high expectations of our pastoral leaders. So when it come to the, "What should we do?" question, we're really only looking at you. We need you to be like Moses: head up the mountain for a chat with God and then come down with the perfect plan. Just don't be gone as long as Moses was. We need an answer this Sunday.

Whether pastors feel this pressure from us or unnecessarily take it onto themselves, they're a breed that's always looking for answers. Conference notebooks squeeze into their bookshelves alongside hundreds of volumes offering thousands of ideas. Surely, someone else has done what we need to do—so the hunt is on through somebody's story. The quarry is that elusive magic bullet that will suddenly redirect our well-worn roads onto the superhighway of ministry effectiveness. We really hope we'll wake up tomorrow and be a foot taller. C'mon, Pastor, that's the answer we need!

Of course, some don't seek their answers from others' stories. They prefer to relive their own. In these cases, the new direction for us ends up being the one our pastor lived at his previous location. We did it this way, we started these ministries, we reached these goals, and we became a great church. Honestly, Pastor, when "we" doesn't include us, we start thinking you'd rather be with them. Sure, it's understandable that some of our pastor's illustrations are drawn from a life he lived elsewhere. We don't mind a few stories of the struggles and victories that bring your former friends to mind. But too many such tales, and we start thinking you either want to go to a home that doesn't include us or that you expect us to be what they were.

We're glad you once got to coach a few Goliaths, but we're 5'7", and we were really hoping that you'd teach us how to get into the game.

So what is it we're trying to say? *We're not your last church or the church you've read about.*

You've likely heard the phrase "square peg in a round hole." It's the feeling you get when you don't fit—like when I once found myself in a dance studio. While I wasn't there against my will, I hardly could have been described as comfortable in that setting. I'd given my wife ballroom dancing lessons as a Christmas gift and discovered that I'd have to attend with her. They say a picture is worth a thousand words; well, one photo of that experience would offer a thousand definitions of one word—*awkward*.

When your physical body has never danced in more than forty years of development—partly due to prohibition in my conservative childhood and partly due to no expectation of a latent Michael Jackson gene anywhere in my body—the first steps are likely to be a bit stiff (along with the second and third ones). I found the entire experience to be beyond my comfort zone—and several zones beyond that. I survived, my wife had fun, and today, we occasionally stumble around the kitchen when the music in our heads begins to match.

The thing about square pegs is that they not only don't fit the round hole of your expectations, but the pegs usually get damaged when you keep trying to force the issue. That's what many congregations feel when their pastor wants them to be the same tribe that brought a success story down the street or across the globe. Surely, if we do what they did, we can get what they got . . . right? Well, that could be true if we were just like them and in the place where they were. We're not. Sorry.

Unfortunately, a few past experiences where previous leaders tried to fold up our ankles and smash our wide hips into someone else's story of a great church have left us with more than a few rough edges. In fact, many church folks hate the word "change" because it conjures up memories of the ministries that didn't work or the new approaches that didn't fit. And those failures have a way of leaving their own marks. If you fail often enough, you can't avoid feeling like failures.

As a church consultant, I have to admit that there aren't many pastors with two ministry success stories. While the fellas who can tell stories of the one place where turnaround occurred and a powerful church was established, not many have a second story of a second place. Why? First of all, many don't ever leave the first place, because the idea of starting over with a new group seems exhausting. Who wants to pay those early prices—the long hours, the battles over values, the hard struggles to find the path that finally brought success? But the second reason we have very few repeat stories is that yesterday's victories at Point A rarely translate to tomorrow's challenges at Point B. In fact, when you interview the rare church leader who has helped build two great congregations, you'll discover that he or she didn't take the same steps in both locations. People and places are significant variables and will keep your "same song, second verse" approach from being a musical masterpiece. Of course, if you haven't successfully written that first one yet, don't be surprised by our unwillingness to simply do what someone else once did. Most congregations have been forced into those dance lessons before.

Pastor, to lead us to better days, you'll need to know who we are, where we've been, and you'll need to gain some understanding of this place where we currently find ourselves. Work with *us*! Yes, all those books and yesterday's stories prove it can be done, but they don't provide a stone-free path for how to do it. Our amazing Creator has shown his vast imagination in making us unique. Our collection of individual gifts and passions, coupled with the specific challenges and opportunities of our community, means that there is a one-of-a-kind journey we have to figure out. Help us find that, Pastor. We aren't what they were, no matter who the "they" might be; and the more you talk about someone else somewhere else, the more we think you'd rather be there.

Though my basketball career ended with only a few minutes of actual playing time, I learned a lot about the game from my location on the bench and ended up coaching a few teams later in life. One thing I learned is that you can't really design your offense, plan your defense, or draw up any real plays until you've seen the team. A strategy built on a dominating rebounder likely won't work if everyone on your team looks like me.

Frankly, there are some things we just weren't made to do.

I can't blow a bubble with chewing gum. There it is: my confession of physiological dysfunction. I've tried so many times, wrangling my tongue around a malleable wad of the pink stuff until a pocket was made ready for my thrust of air. I've blown until my cheeks threatened to rupture. I've blown so hard that I've occasionally had to retrieve my gum from across the room, apologizing to those horrified by its sudden intrusion into their water glasses, hair, or office paperwork. I've been coached by the best, instructed by gum aficionados, watched YouTube instructional videos, and was even mentored by my granddaughters. Still, I found no success—not even an accidental pop. I'm pretty sure I stood alone in this incompetency in elementary school. I regularly set the curve in math class, but even the kids who wore flip flops on test days to aid their counting could blow bubbles. Everyone could . . . everyone, that is, except me.

Now, you may be laughing at my misfortune or sitting with mouth agape at the thought that someone can't do something so easy. But I can't. Today, when my wife offers me a stick of gum to aid the smell of my breath, I reach for a mint instead. I've yet to find any brand of gum with such good flavor that it's worth reliving my childhood trauma.

In the local church, there are some things a pastor thinks everyone should be able to do. The new program is so easy. The assignment is something anyone can do. Look, even the tiny church down the street can do that. *C'mon, you guys—what's wrong with you?* Fact is, there are some things that we can't do well. As the new pastor in Wichita, I felt like the list of what we couldn't do was six pages longer than the one that listed our abilities. As an aging congregation, we didn't have a lot of energy. Things like outreaches and service projects were dreamed in full-color glory in our hearts, but the black-and-white reality was that our hands and feet couldn't get the job done.

When it came to music, we had limits, too. Our youth pastor did well on the guitar, and a fella from Brazil had sufficient rhythm to man the drums, but the twelve-year-old operating the overhead projectors couldn't keep up, and whoever was making the transparencies seemed to have a spelling problem. We were okay and doing our best, but the megachurch a few blocks away looked like a room full of Grammy winners compared to us.

Our teaching ministries weren't strong. We had some good teachers, but they'd asked for a break more than a year ago. Some of their replacements were more willing than able. We loved the few children we had, but had to pay a young woman $20 each week to manage our three-baby nursery. We simply didn't have the congregational energy to do it ourselves.

I know the word "can't."

I've sat through amazing seminars and applauded the kingdom production of great speakers at denominational events. I've heard their stories, purchased their books, and taken notes on their ideas. But when I'd look up from my scribbling of the next idea that would transform our church, all I could see were the faces of my wonderful but weary church friends. So I'd quickly write CAN'T across the new idea and toss the paper toward the growing pile in the corner.

Whatever change you bring has to somehow connect with your people, just like it does with you.

I quickly realized that, if we were going to engage the new day we dreamed of and the change journey to get there, we needed answers that fit us. Somehow, we had to find what *we* could do—because we were the only ones we had to do it with. You see, Pastor, sometimes that old excuse, "We've never done it that way before," is a phony front for the much deeper resistance that admits, "We're afraid we don't have what it takes to do that." People seldom say that one out loud; but if your new idea fits your old church, or a church you've read about, that doesn't mean it will fit the new one.

Whatever change you bring has to somehow connect with your people, just like it does with you. They need the new direction to be a place in which they can invest their passion, reveal their abilities, and give hope to the needs of their community. If they can't do these things well, your new direction probably won't bring the results others have achieved—and if they can't do it well, they may choose not to try. I haven't chewed gum in more than a decade.

Please understand that they're not resisting you with their negative attitudes. Not at all! When they say, "There are just some things we weren't made to do," they're asking you to believe in them. They're asking you to take a long, hard look at the sheep gathered inside your fence and believe that they can be a part of something great. Their story may or may not land you a book deal or a few prominent speaking engagements, but there's a story God has designed for them and they want to find it . . . and they really want your help. So what do you see in them? If their strengths don't match those of other places, where *do* they fit? Maybe other people's stories can stir a few ideas for them, but that's the point—they need to be their own.

Maybe you'll find some answers in the "wins" they've recorded over the years. Remember that history book they tried to get you to read? There are a few stories in there that might remind them of what they're good at. When you're looking for ideas, those are the ones they usually think of, because if it worked before. . . .

Of course, a pastor knows that yesterday often struggles to fit tomorrow, but the victories that were worth writing down may reveal something about the heart of this congregation. Methods change and require regular updating. Passions live a lot longer. When you know your congregation's heartbeat, choosing a path for change becomes much easier and your odds of success skyrocket. But you have to get your head out of those success books and start watching your people. Believe me, I know. . . .

It took me a full year before I happened upon an understanding of our congregation's passion. Actually, it had become obvious much sooner, but some pastors are stubborn. While the list of what we were no longer able to do remained lengthy, I could see one thing we wanted to do really well: I watched my dear friends love people passionately. Guests were ambushed with an enthusiasm that needed some polishing, but there was no denying the heart of these wonderful people. They wanted to wrap their arms around anyone and everyone that might even think about joining our little family.

So we did, and the rest became a pretty wonderful history.

Truth is, Pastor, how you see your people will have a major impact on the quality of your ministry life, and even your own family relationships during your time as pastor. If you view your congregation through the lenses of "can't" and "don't," you'll find yourself lusting for a different church family. That word "lusting" got your attention, didn't it? At its core, lust germinates from the desire for what we don't have, and it can "go to seed" when we break the rules in trying to obtain it. Ultimately, lust says that we want something else, whether that desire is fixated on money, sex, possessions, or, yes, even people.

No, it's not a sin to start a sentence with, "I wish I had someone who could do . . ." Most of us have dreams that are dependent on skills that haven't entered our building yet. But if our sentence multiplies—if we maintain a focus on "who we don't have" and "what we can't do" because of it, contentment will elude us. Now, I don't mean to pile on, but lust has a first cousin called covetousness. He shows up when we see that someone else has what we've been wanting. Some other pastor has the worship team we wish we had, the financial supporters we've often hoped for, or the ministry leaders we know could take us to the next level. Lusting wants someone else; coveting craves their someones.

Such dissatisfaction with our congregation has a way of darkening future thoughts. It's amazing how quickly "we cant's" becomes "we'll nevers." Frustrations mount, people become the problem, and every aspect of ministry life bears the stench of one's polluted frustration. Okay, perhaps that's a bit dramatic. But my work with hundreds of struggling pastors almost always starts with the "them" of their ministry setting. It's hard to imagine how many pastoral resignations travel through these realities not long before the U-Haul is filled. It's the "cant's" and the "wont's" that eat at you. Ministry struggle and perceived failure has a way of nibbling at your sense of self-worth. So when the choice is between "I can't do it" and "I can't do it *here*," the easier decision is to go somewhere else. And if your frustration hasn't spilled over onto your family life, new schools and new friends will certainly provide some impact.

When you see your people through their limitations, you may be missing a better view. That's why I told you that I peeked behind the curtain and discovered that those irritating people weren't exactly what we'd imagined. In virtually every case, I've found that people in local churches genuinely care about the right things, even if their skill sets have yet to find effectiveness. They're waiting for someone themselves. They're waiting for their pastor to believe in them and to celebrate what they *can* do. That's something many congregations want their pastor to know about leading change—*make your plans fit what we can do.*

The antidote for lusting and coveting is always gratitude—the act of celebrating what you already possess. Think it's odd that thanksgiving shows up on most of the "good behavior" lists of the Bible? The apostles don't encourage being thankful because it's a sensible duty or because you may tick God off if you don't demonstrate such manners. They knew that gratitude is an attitude that pushes away those ugly cousins that can only see what's missing. Gratitude reveals a certain type of perspective, but it also helps shape that perspective into the life you really want. Imagine how different life can look when you see people through the list of what they *can* do. How much lighter would your heart be if you were applauding what they do rather than longing for an unlikely performance?

I promise you that such a set of eyes will change everything.

The antidote for lusting and coveting is always gratitude—the act of celebrating what you already possess.

Dorothy could do that. Remember the young Kansas girl whose tornado-powered ride left her in the land of flying monkeys and singing munchkins? Along the path, she encountered three odd characters who were each troubled by what they lacked—a scarecrow lacking a brain, a tin man pining for a heart, and a lion in need of courage. Dorothy had her own issues: more than a bit of homesickness and an angry witch wanting to exact revenge when Dorothy's house chose the witch's sister as its landing spot. But in spite of her desperate desire to get home, Dorothy found inside of herself an ability to give her three traveling companions something they desperately needed: a different view of themselves. She could see that the brainless scarecrow was smarter than he thought. The metal axe man cared deeply about stuff despite his lack of a cardiac organ. And she knew the lion would step up when her moment demanded his rescue. She believed in them when they didn't have reason to share her confidence. Truth is, she gave them more than that wizard guy had to offer.

I've discovered that personally I like change . . . if I get to choose it. But change that's chosen for me can feel threatening—like a referendum on my adequacy. Change has a way of implying that we're currently not enough; so if you're going to lead change effectively, you must find a way to bridge the awkward gap between your people's current value and the place you want to be. We'll talk more about managing the "why" of change in the next chapter, but you must be careful not to imply that your current reality is due to your congregation's inadequacies. Yes, we will grow along a new path; but blaming people for where we're at doesn't get you off to a running start . . . unless you mean running *from them*.

In Wichita, when I discovered what my congregation could do—their love for people and their desire for others to worship with us that seemed to gush uncontrollably from some of them—their faces lit up with self-worth. The discovery that our road forward didn't reject them but was instead paved with the passion that *already beat inside them* made change something to be gladly embraced. "This is what we've always wanted," replaced, "We've never done it this way before." I heard various versions of, "Pastor believes in us" so often that I finally decided I did. And I discovered that belief is what my people were desperate for. They could read the financial statements; they could see the empty chairs and the gray heads that occupied the full ones. It was news to no one that something needed to change, but they needed to believe that a new day—with them in it—was possible.

Frankly, the discovery changed me more than anyone else. When I turned my eyes from the "cant's" to the one "can" I could find in my congregation, I fell in love with the possibilities. I smiled to see senior saints inviting twenty-somethings to lunch and nearly laughed out loud when they said yes. I cheered the old white guy with his arm around a Chinese student. I nearly danced when a deacon decided to roast a goat in his yard because he heard that's how some Africans welcome new friends to their neighborhood. When dozens of Kenyans and Ugandans showed up, I went ahead and danced. I loved it when I invited the congregation to greet each other during our services and felt like I'd never get their attention back. I loved it, and it taught me to love them. And that's probably the biggest reason why they followed me in our journey of change.

You see, if you don't love them, I'm not sure they'll want you changing them. But when you satisfy that need for genuine affirmation and they see signs of your devotion and overhear your statements of pride in them (when you didn't know they could hear you), well, they'll quickly be ready to get started on that new road you see for them. So you see, Pastor, when they say make your plans fit what we can do, that's really what *both* of us need.

So how does one determine a congregation's true skill set? Certainly there are a variety of approaches you can use. Some find the church's capacity in its history, while others simply learn from the perspective of more experienced folks on the leadership team. You can engage an assessment tool—and there are many of those that can help you identify strengths— or you can prayerfully trust your own eyes, looking for places where joy and productivity seem most abundant. Regardless of your approach to learning your people's abilities, there are a couple of critical thoughts to be added to your perspective.

First, believe that strengths exist. I can almost hear someone's insistence that their folks possess no real capacity, that excellence isn't anywhere near their grasp on any subject. Like the student whose best subject is lunch, it may seem that there's very little to build on; but trust me, there's something to find. You may have to dig deeper, but remember that you're pasturing God's sheep, and no one wants you to succeed more than He does.

Lay aside the things you and your people truly can't do. You'll get to them soon enough.

Second, keep in mind that your real calling is to help this church find its path rather than to steer it into someone else's. Just as God equips individuals uniquely for His work, He also gathers a collection of those unique abilities into a congregation that reflects His amazing creativity. There are some things we're made to do, and a few that we really can't quite yet. Find the road for your people and you'll see them come to life in new ways.

Lay aside the things you and your people truly can't do. You'll get to them soon enough. Keep in mind that, as you do what your church family does well, you'll draw in the people who can do what you currently can't. Focus on your strengths, and God will bring answers to your current weaknesses. Remember, He's the One who proves strong in the midst of our weak spots.

Finally, be patient. Until the answers come into view, keep pouring your energies into loving and learning your congregation. The deeper such relationships and knowledge grow, the better equipped you'll be for leading change in the days ahead.

So Pastor, let me remind you that *we're not your last church or the church you've read about*, and every time you wish we were, we get a little further from your heart. Keep in mind that *there are just some things we weren't made to do*. Just like the square peg, we get a bit more damaged every time you push us toward things that don't fit. We're asking you to *make your plans fit what we can do*. That's when we can feel successful, and that's when we begin making real progress together.

Never forget that God is on your side. I was stunned to see how God began to transform that little Wichita church. When we started loving people—you know, that thing we thought we were made to do—God started bringing people for us to love. Honestly, He did all the heavy lifting. All we had to do was give our best to the path He had designed us to engage.

CHAPTER FIVE

PATH . . .

Where are we going?

uring my high school years, I hopped into a car with my church friends to attend a state-wide youth convention. The event was being held in the state capitol city of Topeka, some sixty miles west of my home in the suburbs of Kansas City. An hour drive flies by pretty quickly when you're with friends, and soon we were excitedly checking into a high-rise hotel along with youth groups from as far west as the Colorado line. There's nothing quite like the buzz (and the occasional fire alarm) of a Holiday Inn filled with several hundred teenagers.

But not all of our group had arrived yet. My sister and four of her friends hadn't been able to leave with the rest of us. They were set to depart about an hour later than we had, and soon they'd be wheeling into the parking lot, ready to join in the fun—or so we thought. Their scheduled arrival time came and went, soon followed by hour after hour. As the evening wore on, you can imagine the concern that began to escalate among those of us looking for an older girl's car to wheel into the hotel parking garage. We waited . . . and waited . . . and tried to imagine (and not imagine) all of the possible reasons for their delay. Since we were a decade or so from the release of the first mobile phones, answers weren't easily gained. In those days, dinosaur-like contraptions called "pay phones" adorned gas station parking lots in case anyone felt the need to make a phone call. Apparently, neither the driver, my sister, nor any of the three blondes in the back seat thought it necessary.

Finally, around 10:00 p.m.—a full five hours after they were expected—the girls came waving and laughing into the hotel drive. Their mood reflected the same joy we'd all felt when we first arrived, but suffice it to say that their smiles didn't match our current frame of mind. Shouts of "Hi, guys!" were met with "Where (on earth) have you been?"

I'll never forget the response: "Oh, we missed a turn . . . like, you know, back in Kansas City when the highway, like, uh, makes you choose to go this way or that?" Waving hands tried to convey the messages of large directional signs offering the interstate options of west and east. "Well, we went the wrong way." A few follow-up questions revealed that the girls had driven two hours before beginning to discuss their possible error. Thanks to a nice—and I'm sure laughing—man at a gas station near Columbia, Missouri, they turned around and headed back toward Kansas.

Later, I asked the girl who had driven her parent's car on such a long adventure how she had managed to miss the correct sign—the one that says TOPEKA in really big letters—instead turning toward ST. LOUIS. Her response stunned me: "Well, all the other cars were going that way."

Wow.

When the Bible tells us that, "Without vision, people perish," the idea contained helps us acknowledge the sad truth that, in the absence of clear direction, people will go their own way and do their own thing, staying on their self-stylized path even when the evidence insists they should stop. The tragic destination implied by "perish" flows from the writer's original desert context. Frankly, if you wander away on your own in a desert, you die. So we need a clearly-communicated path, a sense of wise direction, a vision that can mark our steps, if we are to avoid such calamity.

The "Where are we going?" question matters in virtually every area of life. We need clear plans on the job, an economic direction to prepare for our futures, and a shared path for our family lives. Without vision in these and many other areas, we wander around until we find ourselves ill-equipped to continue. Frankly, some folks, like that carload of teenage girls, can't manage to stay on the right path even when there are really big signs.

At church, the questions asked by clear vision are no less important:

Why are we here?

Where are we going?

What does Jesus want us to do?

Such queries float like soft whispers just above the people of slowly-diminishing congregations as they drive onto their grass-riddled parking lots and enter their steadily-emptying buildings. Sadly, nobody hears them. Instead, these good folks engage their weekly worship habits, asking a different set of questions:

Who's teaching Tom's class today?

Why haven't the Joneses been here the past few months?

Who moved the piano over there?

And sometimes, *Why are those people sitting in my seat?*

It's not that these saints have forgotten what their local church is really supposed to be all about, but a few years of surviving and maintaining bring their own areas of focus. On a sunny day, when the air flows smoothly into the sails, the crew can marshal their energies along their journey's map; but when storms have you taking on water, managing the seasick, and occasionally watching friends take off in the lifeboats, well, you can understand if we might be a bit off-course.

You see, one truth from the wisdom of church health tells us that lost vision in the pew is a primary cause for plateaued growth and—typically—launches a congregation toward decline. If you're the pastor at a church experiencing such a reality, you're probably sensing a large need to make changes. A critical first step is helping us get our hands on another copy of that map. The last one may have washed overboard.

That's what we're going to discuss in this chapter. We need the "why" returned to its necessary spot of leading the "whats." Before we're ready to do new things, many of us are going to need a better understanding of where we're going. Because Pastor, one of the things we need you to know is that we're probably a little confused about the vision.

Unfortunately, when churches begin journeys toward change, they have the tendency to start in the wrong spot—with needed actions, new programs, or altered behaviors. The motivation toward change is driven by, "Let's do something" or, "Let's do something different," and suddenly we're moving down a new path hoping for a better day. We want to take action—at least, most of us do. We see a need to fix something, and so we grab our ministry wrench and start twisting. Maybe a recent conference has given us a new idea or shown us a few steps we think will work in our church, so we look to "plug and play" our new discovery in hopes that our church can get the same results that the conference speaker seems to be enjoying.

But effective change doesn't start with the "what" of our change. To truly find a new path—the *right path* for our church—the effective starting line must be marked by "where" and "why" questions. Questions like, "Where are we going? Why do we want to go there?"

It may surprise you to learn that, in spite of hearing fifty sermons a year from your Sunday morning pulpit, your congregation may not be entirely clear as to why your church exists and what your mission really is. Now, the problem isn't that they have no idea, but instead that each individual typically has his *own* idea of what the church should do or try to be. As someone has wisely observed, most churches don't drift into the future with no vision. They drift with *di*vision. And in a multitude of ideas and directions, forward movement becomes highly unlikely—or even impossible.

> But effective change doesn't start with the "what" of our change. To truly find a new path—the right path for our church— the effective starting line must be marked by "where" and "why" questions.

One of the primary causes of plateaued growth in a local church's ministries is a lost sense of the vision that once drove them forward. Frankly, after a church has had more than a few pastors and chased after each one's unique and varied vision for the church's future, you can understand how the train might have slipped from the tracks a bit. One pastor's dream of a new building, followed by another's pursuit of attendance numbers, followed by still another's priority on discipleship process, coupled with the next leader's emphasis on community service projects, has left us chasing a lot of different ideas of where we think we're going.

And for every "where" question, there can be multiple "why" explanations. Maybe one pastor wanted us to be the strongest church in the city, while another thought making disciples was a one-at-a-time task. Of course, a few may have driven us forward thinking that the church's growth looked good on their resume, while still others hungered for worldwide impact through a focus on missions. The list of possible "why" responses that can dot a church's journey are more plenteous than the number of fast food restaurants along your nearby interstate.

When we say that the people might need help with vision, we're not implying that they've somehow lost their spiritual bearings or started ignoring Jesus' command to "Go and make disciples." In truth, they have likely heard that command interpreted into a myriad of past initiatives, so the road forward looks more like a trampled field than a clear path.

Pastor, your first step on this journey of change is to help us find the "where" and "why" of your church's very existence. Now, you may think that you preached about that once and that they all should remember, but the truth is that clear vision requires a bit more of a process. They need to find the right destination for their church and the ways to get there that fit who they are.

Imagine if you could capture the full passion of our local church leaders into a single circle. Yes, that's right! Put every dream, every thought of success, every priority that we believe should drive our ministry efforts at our church, into a congealed ball like this one:

Our desperation to see lives changed, to invest in the next generation, to make a difference in our communities, to preserve and defend our faith, to love people unconditionally, to teach Jesus' truth until folks begin to live it, and a whole lot of other treasured passions are somehow fitted into that orb, making it burst with possibilities. Maybe we should have added a fuse, 'cause all that passion is ready to explode within those who've stepped forward to help lead your church.

Now, suppose we bounce another ball into the equation. This time, let's fill that circle with the abilities which are proven to reside within our congregation. Let's imagine that all the things we do well—and the stuff we're getting better at—are crammed inside this:

We're really good at outreach events, or maybe our strength is our musical talent. Some churches have amazing teachers, while others are simply some of the friendliest folks in the country. Truth is, even in the smallest places, there are capacities for excellence, and most of us know what they are—or perhaps what they aren't.

Now, understand something about ability: it's not always associated with activity. Just because someone can do something doesn't mean they are currently doing it. And clearly, the fact that someone is doing something doesn't necessarily indicate the ability to do it *well*. Many local church volunteers volunteered to do what they do. Willing people are a wonderful gift to any pastor, but willing people with ability are an even greater prize.

You might find it interesting to know that most plateaued or declining congregations are very busy. In fact, they tend to be doing more things than their healthy, growing counterparts. I once asked a group of small church pastors and their leadership teams to list the various outreach efforts their churches attempted in a single year. One team handed me a list with twenty-three unique efforts enumerated. I was impressed. Surely any church doing that much to reach others has to be growing . . . right?

When I asked concerning their church size, I was surprised to learn that this team represented a congregation of around forty worshippers each week. Most of us know that, at church, about 20% of the people do 80% of the work, so I did the math. Likely, eight people were carrying this enormous load, and I was guessing that the five ladies sitting at that pastor's table were among them. They looked tired, and one lady even looked a bit bitter. I assumed that was his wife.

Most healthy, growing churches have figured out what they do well, and they spend their energies there. They don't try to do everything and they don't assume that busyness is a sign of effectiveness. Instead, they target ministry efforts that fit the abilities God has given them, and they give those strengths 100% of their effort. Activity and ability aren't siblings in most churches. In fact, they're not even third cousins in a few congregations. So before you go filling up this second ball with everything you're doing, make sure you're *really good* at what you do.

Let's add one more circle to our story. This time, let's accumulate the needs of the community in which we're located. Imagine pouring all of the need that surrounds us into a ball like this:

It's hard to imagine getting all of that need into such a tiny circle, isn't it? Most of us are surrounded by brokenness, poverty of all types, abuse, damaged relationships, job uncertainty, depravity, spiritual emptiness—and that's just on one neighborhood block. Add in all that's going on at the local high school, the stories no one's big enough to tell at the daycare center, the turmoil over at the production plant, and the fear that fills our local hospital rooms, and the amount of need is overwhelming. Remember, even Jesus felt the immensity of the needs lining up in front of Him everyday, and He could do amazing things with just a few pieces of bread or a handful of mud.

Now, remember that we're searching for our vision: the "where" that we believe our church is designed to reach. So let's take those three circles and push them together into something like this:

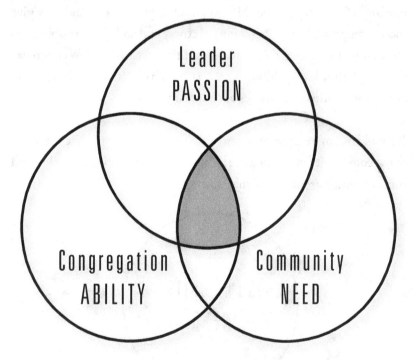

Do you see that shaded slice in the middle—the place where our three circles overlap? That's where you'll find your church's intended vision. It's where passion, ability, and need intersect, and it's likely the critical spot your congregation has been looking for—maybe for a long time.

So, Pastor, help them find that. If you want to lead them in a journey of change, they'll be much better equipped for a path that's headed in the best direction. You see, this is a direction you can lead then in because it's a big piece of your passion; and they can join you because this road fits their abilities. Of course, your community will respond to this vision as well because, together, your team has connected with something they desperately need.

In fact, if your vision doesn't connect strongly with these three circles and everything they contain, your people can't go where you want them to go. Why should they follow you if they can't see your passion for the trip? How can they possibly get there if they lack the necessary abilities? And why should they even bother if they're not meeting the needs of those around them? If you're going to make the vision clear, these are the pieces they need to be able to fully grasp.

And while you're helping us renew our vision, we may need you to *reinforce our grasp of what's truly important.* The passion and priorities of a local church rightly run on biblical values. After all, our congregation intends to be a local piece of Jesus' Church. That's why they started (however many years ago) and that's the main reason why they gather every week—even if you may not recognize Him in their current performance. They want to be what He wants and to lay claim to the promise that the "gates of hell" cannot stop their pursuit.

Please remember that you're the only one who hangs out at the church every day. The rest of your congregation travels other hallways.

Now, please understand and be gracious as you view their apparent values. You see, they function in a climate of very different values six days each week, and sometimes that different slate intrudes on their "day seven" lives as well. So when you see selfishness or pursuit of comfort in their attitudes and behaviors, they need you to recognize their need for a stronger grasp of God's priorities. Surely, you can understand that they are heavily influenced by their employers' values, those taught by their entertainment choices, and the occasionally dysfunctional ones they inherited from their families of origin. If they're going to be the church you want them to be, they're going to need the "whys" of their ministry efforts consistently highlighted. The mission Jesus assigned to all of us—to make disciples of all nations, baptizing them and teaching them His truth—isn't always first in their thoughts on Tuesdays, or Thursdays, or any of those days that don't find them in your pews. They are called upon to live by other missions, and have become accustomed to Sunday boundaries for their spiritual pursuits.

Such compartmentalization is highly unhealthy for your congregation, but it's where your people most commonly live. In fact, it's far more natural for their weekday values to slip into their Sunday thinking than it is for it to happen in the opposite direction. If you expect them to live by the twofold priority of loving God and loving others, you'll have to fuel those desires intentionally so they can choose to live them. Please remember that you're the only one who hangs out at the church every day. The rest of your congregation travels other hallways.

Values are the core of church effectiveness. While vision helps us know where we want to go, values are the reasons we go there. A family may decide to make Grandma's house their destination on Saturday, but they do so because they love Grandma, they can't resist her cookies, or they treasure the way she spoils them. Her house is the destination, but her love for them and their love for her are the reasons for the trip. Without these reasons, the four-hour drive would feel more like duty—if they bothered to make the trip at all. Values work the same way at church. When the "why" of our efforts is unclear or undeveloped in our hearts, the activities and ministry strategies you introduce will lack necessary motivation. Activities that lack vision and a clear sense of our priorities end up making us feel like we're driving around with no destination. We need to know where we're going and *why* we want to go there if you want to see our best effort.

Any change that lacks a connection to clear vision and values will likely fail. New strategies void of real reason-for-being lack the needed energy to be sustained. As you can see, your people really need the "why" before they're ready to hear the "what."

———————————————————————

Funny thing about values—they can be really difficult to change. Someone said that changing values typically takes a generation, and I think he died before we could change his mind. The idea behind such a disappointing statement is that our values are shaped both by how we are raised and as a reaction to how we are raised. So we carry some of mom and dad's list, and we have some values that are products of our determined effort to do things differently than they did. You can probably think of a few of these items in your own life; but the point is that, if you expect people to change, you'll likely have better luck with their kids. Values don't change . . . easily.

The guy who sharply confronts a hat-wearing teenager on Sunday mornings isn't going to quickly buy into your new *come-as-you-are* focus. Those who are horrified at the rise of cohabiting couples in the community will struggle mightily with your idea of "love them until we can lead them." Today, our kids are stunned at the stupidity of racism, but our parents might still be holding onto such thoughts. Generational conflicts at church are the product of differing values, and sadly, it seems like one of the generations has to either leave or die off for those issues to be fully resolved.

But things don't have to be so hopeless. In fact, Pastor, there's something we want you to know. We'll more likely act our way into new thinking than think our way into new actions.

Let me introduce you to Tim (not his real name, but his story really happened). Tim and his wife Sandy (not her real name either) had been long-time members of their congregation, a worship community that had become home to people from more than fifty different nations. That diversity had never excited Tim. In fact, he was highly resistant to "those" people, especially the ones whose skin color would typically be labeled "black."

But Tim and Sandy's Sunday school teacher embraced and really enjoyed the cultural variety. So did Sandy, though her occasional efforts to discuss such feelings with Tim had taught her *not* to discuss such feelings with Tim. So when the Sunday school class decided to start an Adopt-A-Student program, in which local families would become a "family" for some of the church's international college students, Sandy signed them up (helping Tim learn not to skip Sunday school class in the future). Now, the teacher was unaware of Tim's long-held attitudes toward people of color, so she handed Sandy the names of two girls from the African continent. When Tim learned of their new assignment ... let's just say that the ensuing conversation helped Sandy know her husband's feelings quite clearly. "You can do what you want, but count me OUT!"

However, one Sunday, Sandy invited the girls to join them for lunch. She and their teenage daughter engaged the moment enthusiastically while Tim sat quietly, waiting to pay the bill. Over the next several weeks, lunch dates expanded into movie nights, ball games, and any other slice of Americana Sandy could think of. And things really began to change for Tim. His fascination with these two girls grew. He found himself wanting to learn about their home countries and the families who had bravely sent them so many miles for educational opportunities. By the end of the first semester, Tim and Sandy had hosted an event for all the international students in their own home, and they were spending more time with their "adopted" daughters than any of the other church families.

Tim's attitude toward others completely changed, and Tim completely changed with it. Today, he's among the first to greet guests at his local church, especially if they appear different from the small town world he grew up in. In fact, if you met him, you'd list him as one of the last people you'd expect to have once harbored racist ideals. He's just not that guy anymore . . . *at all*!

What changed Tim? His actions—or, more specifically, the actions Sandy lured him into—opened the door for changed thinking. Quite honestly, I'm convinced that you could have argued the agenda of political correctness with Tim until he lay on his future deathbed and never won the debate. But put a few easy and compelling steps in front of him, and you have a whole new man in less than three months.

Thinking produces actions, but actions can produce new thinking. So when you decide that your congregation's values need changing, look for actions that can serve as handles for people to latch onto in that endeavor.

If you do, you'll see a real change in values occur within months rather than decades.

When you decide that your congregation's values need changing, look for actions that can serve as handles for people to latch onto in that endeavor.

If your people struggle with inward focus (the most prominent reason for church decline), take them to the neighborhoods of the hurting, let them walk beside you in hospital hallways, or invite them to sit with you at Friday night's high school football game. Expose them to the church's real mission field so you have real-life images to stand alongside your preaching fervor. There's nothing quite like a need to help someone find the energy for new actions. Until Tim found himself sitting at a restaurant table with two African girls, he had never had a reason to reconsider his long-held values. New experiences open new doors for all of us. "Well, I never . . ." is usually the product of an actual "never." When we haven't engaged certain situations or opportunities, we find ourselves suspicious or even fearful of what such circumstances are truly all about. Until I visited another country and worshipped with those from a completely different cultural context, I had my ideas about such settings, but no real knowledge of them. After that first visit, my whole world changed. You might say my perspective grew bigger as my feet got a little further from home. Now, I love such learning experiences and can't wait 'til the next one.

For many of the people you lead, Pastor, new ideas are just that—new! You can't expect their values to incorporate experiences they've never had (or haven't had for a while). You're going to have to stretch their legs before you can expect them to open their minds. New programs and outreach ideas may look like the road to a new day for our local church, but the real wins pile up when you help us align our vision and values to the priorities Jesus intends for His Church. That vision and those values are the *real* source of Monday-to-Saturday behaviors that will transform our congregation and our individual lives. So give us the "why" before the "what" and show us some ways to practice the attitudes you want us to develop.

Then, *we'll need you to live those values with us.*

Those who say, "A picture is worth a thousand words," understand the power of illustration. We may hear things we don't fully understand, but when we can *see* and *watch* them, those ideas become clear. Maybe it's the fact that I've lived in Missouri on three different occasions, but I've become a firm believer in the need for you to "show me" the kind of person you want me to be.

Pastors talk a lot. That's okay—it's their job to do so. We *expect* a pastor to talk to us, uninterrupted, for about thirty minutes on a weekly basis. He can talk for longer, but most of us get our fill in the first half hour—if he'd stop then, we'd probably like him a bit more. But the point is that we pay him to talk. And there's a lot for him to talk about. The Bible provides sixty-six literary masterpieces crammed full of the stuff we need for life, and we instinctively know that, over his expected forty-five to fifty-year career, he won't come close to covering it all. There's more material than he can provide for us to assimilate into our weeks, yet we're glad that he continues to press forward.

But no sermons speak as loudly as the ones we see our pastor *live*. His appeals for us to love others drive deeper into our psyches when we see him loving someone beyond the church setting. His calls for us to worship God go down more easily when we get a glimpse of what that looks like by watching him. When he demands that we love our wives, seeing him caring for his own wife when he didn't know we were watching shouts volumes. And when it comes to the best values, people learn them more quickly when they see those values in your life. You teach them to be friendly by being friendly, you show them how to pray when you pray, and you help them love their neighbors by taking a plate of cookies to the people who live across the street from the parsonage.

Disciples don't follow a creed or a list of behavioral guidelines. They follow a person.

Now, as a church grows larger, the amount of actual contact a pastor has with his congregation and his community seems to diminish. He can't make every hospital call or be the centerpiece of the church's visitation program. He may not be able to shake every hand this Sunday or be the needed counselor for every struggling church member. In fact, as the crowd grows, Pastor may seem to be more of a messenger of truth for lives he rarely sees lived. And if his opportunities to live with his people are growing fewer, then their opportunities to watch him live are shrinking, too. When the pursuit of values devolves into a "do as I say" paradigm rather than a "watch what I do" paradigm, the goal will never be reached. Avoiding such a destination demands that a pastor step beyond his adopted scheduling strategies so he can live with some of his people and help them see how they are to live. Disciples don't follow a creed or a list of behavioral guidelines. They follow a person.

Now, I'm not suggesting that you find ways to perform for your people. Instead, if you want to guide your people toward new values, become the person you want them to be. Let the truth of your Sunday morning text rewrite *your* programming. Practice the steps you prescribe for others. Live the truth you seem so passionate about when the microphones are on.

Sometimes, you need to respond to your own altar call.

And when you do, you show us how to live by the same passion that led you to your proposed ideas for change. When our hearts beat as one and our feet chase the same direction, we'll better understand where you want us to go, what you want us to do, and why you're so convinced that we should. Telling us where to go is never quite as much fun as traveling there together.

So before we dive a bit deeper into the concept of living together, let us remind you of the things we've asked you to consider as you lead us in change:

First, remember that *we're probably a little confused about the vision.* We've chased more than one of those over the years, so we probably aren't as clear as you think we should be on the direction you want for our church. There's a much-needed security in knowing where we're going, and we may be able to offer a few ideas for how to get there if you'll help us better understand the Promised Land that motivates our trudge through the desert.

Second, *reinforce our grasp of what's truly important.* Yes, we've heard a truckload of sermons extolling the identities and virtues of discipleship priorities, but we need your help to pick through that load for the greatest treasures. Our values will ultimately determine where we are headed and how we behave along the way, so keep the best ones in front of us regularly. Until we're feeling the same "whys," we're not likely to give our best to the "whats" of ministry action.

And about those values: don't forget that they can be really difficult to change. One sermon, or even a dozen, won't easily bring a new day to our lives or our church. Every day is a battle to keep right priorities in focus. Without your help, we'll likely let the cultural agendas that surround us gain a foothold on our Sunday thinking. Please be patient and gracious with us, and believe that we can be the people we want to be. We really need you to believe in us if we're ever going to believe in ourselves.

We're more likely to act our way into new thinking than to think our way into new actions. Sermons alone will never achieve heart change. We need your words, but we also need you to offer practical steps, to exemplify the goals of those words. Telling us we should do something without showing us how to do it won't develop us as disciples. You wouldn't want your surgeon to have been trained that way, would you? Teach us how to live with a few actions that can grow into new ways of thinking.

And finally, *we need you to live those values with us.* Let us feel the power of your example. If we can step into your footprints, we're more likely to go where you're going. Like the coxswain who shouts to the men at the oars, help us see that you're in the boat with us.

If you can give us clarity on the "where" and the "why" of our congregational journey, the "what" will be easier to choose and achieve. But change that lacks clear vision and connection to values is just a bunch of new stuff to add to our already-busy lives.

CHAPTER SIX

PATTERN . . .

Seeing is . . . doing.

P erhaps you've heard the ancient saying, "Once a man, twice a child." The clever quip, quoted as far back as Sophocles (450 BC) and borrowed more recently as a title for a John Lennon biography, actually has several meanings. Some use it to describe the foibles of a so-called "mid-life crisis," while others lament their man's unwillingness to grow up. But Shakespeare probably used the idea best in Hamlet when describing how old age tends to bring back many of the characteristics of childhood. We must be cared for as children in our earliest years and then we return to such need after a few decades of adult life. I guess that's something to look forward to, right?

Somehow, I have decided that a symptom of this transition is one's fascination with assembling puzzles. My granddaughters rate puzzles as a top-five favorite activity, trailing only coloring, dancing, and playing house—staples in their preferred daily agenda. At age three, my oldest princess mastered a 50-state puzzle, even assembling the tiny northeast pieces without the help of a grandparent (thus allowing Papa's geography limitations to remain hidden awhile longer). Interestingly enough, I can recall that my grandparents were puzzle aficionados, too. In the years that this granddad has yet to reach, they would take on challenges of the 500, 1000, or even 1500-piece variety. Then, once completed, special adhesive was added, a frame purchased, and soon a lovely pastoral scene was added to the living room wall. Who knew that art came in a box? So whether or not one is twice a child or not, it seems we are, at least, twice a fan of puzzles.

In my younger years I gave puzzles a try, too. Like many kids, I thought my grandparents were cool, so I joined in their fun. I quickly learned that the key to puzzle assembly is the picture on the box lid. If you can see what the end product is supposed to look like, your odds of achieving a satisfactory final result are greatly enhanced. No picture, and you're not likely to achieve wall art status. Instead, frustrations multiply and precious hours of childhood are wasted indoors, slaving over a table, seeking achievement that won't impress anybody but your grandparents.

You need the box lid.

Frankly, Pastor, if your congregation is going to achieve the goals of your vision and become the people your ministry dream requires, they need that lid, too. Somehow, some way, they need you to do more than tell them what the puzzle of their lives is supposed to look like.

We need you to show us.

Honestly, assembling our lives is more difficult than a great many boxed puzzles. Most of us are working from a disadvantage or two. We don't have all the pieces and some of the ones in our box are broken or don't seem to fit together as easily as want them to fit. Someone has wisely observed that people "don't come to church in whole pieces anymore"— an observation that reveals the damage and dysfunction that has crept into nearly every family on some level. The world of *Leave it to Beaver's* Ward and June Cleaver has crumbled into the world of *Modern Family*: a world in which many have stopped by counselors, rehab centers, and divorce lawyers on their way to church. Finding folks whose lives remain unscathed by relationship hurt, failed choices, or abuse is about as easy as a *Where's Waldo* page. So while they absolutely want the life you and Jesus talk about, finding the life change that's possible—and every other change journey you want them to walk with you—is going to require a picture. They need to see it, and it'll help them a lot if they can see it in you.

Don't just tell us what to do, but show us what it looks like.

In the previous chapter, we touched briefly on the idea of modeling the desired change. But this is no minor issue. In fact, it demands its own chapter, because even the best motivational speeches won't produce desired behavior nearly as effectively as a clear snapshot of the targeted result.

One can easily see that we have become a culture of visual learners. While the phrase "a picture is worth a thousand words" is at least nearly a century old,[1] modern folks have lost all interest in the thousand words; they demand a picture if they're going to pay attention to you at all. That's why cool pastors like you enhance your sermons with videos and outline

---

1   Printer's Ink, "One look is worth a thousand words," December 1921.

slides. You know that the ears have lost their powers of retention, but the eyes apparently still have it. Show us a picture or paint a picture in our minds and we can get on board with your ideas. Limiting us to just your words is like staring at a box of jumbled puzzle pieces, wondering if the effort required will prove worthwhile, or even possible. In life, as in puzzle assembly, people need a picture of the intended result. And if you're going to lead them to be different than they are, that's one thing they need you to know, Pastor. *Don't just tell us what to do, but show us what it looks like.*

The life of the modern pastor has become quite complicated. Books that chronicle the unrealistic expectations placed upon these spiritual shepherds could likely fill a room at the Library of Congress. Virtually every list of most stressful occupations includes "pastor" in the top five. It's a job that the faint of heart should never engage.

You see, we need a lot from our pastors:

- We need them to feed us with God's truth in a way that holds our attention—no easy task among those who need a commercial break every few minutes, even when what we're watching requires little concentration.

- We need pastors who understand us and have secret strategies to help us overcome the stuff that seems to always be overcoming us. These counselors must provide more than an ear for our troubles; they must also discover a road map out of our troubles—and we would prefer that the journey be as easy as possible.

- We need pastors who can keep the church well-organized. We tend to notice anything and everything that might be a bit out of place, and we're more than willing to point out untended dust or the hiccups in the flow of our worship services.

- We want our pastor to be a highly spiritual leader as well. He should pray like some of the great ones of the past. Didn't I read that Martin Luther prayed three hours a day? That sounds like a good plan to me.

- We also want pastor to implement the great ideas that God reveals to us in various moments. After all, our brother-in-law's church is doing some really great things, and there's no reason why our church can't do those things, too. So we need pastor to pull a team together. And stay ready, 'cause we'll think of another idea soon.

- Of course, pastor must raise the funds needed to keep our church doors open and our ministries humming. We need pastor to be good at that, especially since we want him to get more of this money from others than from us.

- Pastor must be relationally engaging. Each of us wants to be close to him and his family. At the same time, we need his to be a model family: his kids can play with our kids, but we expect his will need little supervision due to the superior parenting skills of those who live in parsonages.

- We need pastor to represent our church well in our city. He should love the church's neighbors for us, become friends with the mayor for us, understand and strategize to meet the needs of our community for us, and be a voice for righteousness amidst the secular evils that surround us.

- Of course, we will need pastor's immediate attention to our moments of crisis. His light must always be on so he can respond quickly to our visits to the emergency room, the principal's office, and certainly the mortuary. When we're in need, he's the one we need. So please don't send the associate pastor.

- And he should have time to read and respond to my Facebook posts, since he really only works that one day each week.

Sounds reasonable, doesn't it?

Without question, our expectations of pastors need a bit of trimming. Psychologists tell us that pastors tend to carry more than three times the amount of stress that those who sit in their congregations are trying to manage. Somebody should fix that. But Pastor, one thing we need you to know about leading change is that unfair expectations work both ways.

After that last list, you may doubt whether pastors could possibly be guilty of similar unfairness, but consider some of the expectations pastors seem to have of their congregations:

- We need our people to engage our worship services with energy and enthusiasm, regardless of the sixty hours they worked this past week or the crying baby that kept them awake throughout most of Saturday night.
- We need our people to know just what to say after our Sunday message so we can feel affirmed in our efforts—and we would rather them stifle their discomforts so it will be easier to keep everyone happy.
- We want our people to open their homes to small groups, to stay after church dinners for clean up, to volunteer for Vacation Bible School, and to change their vacation plans so they can join our missions trips.
- We need our people to fill all the ministry spots in our expansive plan, even though they also have to work overtime, coach the kids' ballgames, and do their part with the P.T.A.
- We need our people to be friendly to our Sunday guests and roll out the proverbial red carpet so people they've never met will sit by them in next week's service, too.

- We need our people to share our passion for church growth, in spite of their recognition that we're not keeping up with the needs of the folks already attending.

- Of course, we need the people to fund the vision pounding in our hearts. With missionaries regularly parading through our pulpits and building campaigns to rally us toward a greater future, money is desperately needed for the mission, and it can only come from one source: the people. In many a pastor's eyes, faithfulness to God is principally measured by filling seats and filling offering buckets.

- We'd appreciate everyone avoiding emergencies on our much-needed days off . . . and if we could start getting two weeks' notice for funerals, that'd be great!

This list, like the previous one, could be longer. But the most unrealistic expectation a pastor can inadvertently require of his people is to understand what he's talking about every time he talks.

You see, Pastor, you went to seminary or have spent hours in your study, thinking about what every verse in the Bible means for daily life. You have stacks of commentaries and seem to know the church fathers personally. So when you preach, you fill the auditorium with amazing ideas and compel people to live God's eternal purposes, even on their mundane Tuesdays. You motivate and motivate and motivate them with your challenges, and they shout "amens" in agreement. But if you don't show them what the action steps look like, things won't happen, no matter how compelling your argument might be.

Keep in mind that they attend your local church willingly. They get up early on what may be the only non-working day of their week and put on clothing they'd rather not wear for long so they can sit in your services, while lakes go unfished and grandmas go unvisited. No one makes them wrestle their kids into church clothes and hope they'll behave in your building (because people will whisper about them if they don't). They do this voluntarily, because they want what you're saying. They want to be the people of God who demonstrate His superior form of living and live in His blessings. They want to fulfill His purposes and find the abundant life Jesus hinted at for them. They want this so much that they will regularly give half of their weekend days to pursuing it in your pews, scribbling your words on the back of your bulletins, and resolving that this week will be a better one than the one they just finished.

But they need you to connect the dots for them. Compelling words of challenge and motivation aren't sufficient. We need to know how to live, how to engage your vision, and how to reach our neighbors—by watching you do it! You see, Pastor, it's the things you do that they know *really* matter to you. Since you fill their ears for nearly an hour, nearly fifty times a year, the moments in which your words startle them to action are likely getting fewer and further between. But when their eyes behold what your feet and hands are doing, suddenly, they have something more to hold onto. They may not always do what you say, but they get excited when they can do what you're doing.

You see, Pastor, it's the things you do that they know really matter to you.

Over the long haul, your people are going to become what you are. That's the nature of following your leadership. They will care for what you care about. They will do what you do with them. So show them what you think they should be doing, and you will greatly increase the likelihood of them doing it.

They understand when your expectations of them may go overboard a bit. Frankly, they know that they do that to you at times, too. But please understand that the most unrealistic idea you can have about your congregation is that they can put your words into action without seeing those actions in you. They'll follow you into spiritual battle and give their last ounces of strength to the eternal agenda you lay before them, but the only way they will truly know what to do is by watching you.

Closely related to the idea of watching you live the vision is the question of how long they'll get to watch you do it. You see, Pastor, one of the things your people want you to know about leading change is that we need you to stay long enough to help us reach the targeted destination. Ministry transition is a complex reality to process. Now, a small section within a chapter like this one isn't the place to explore the full range of such issues, nor their impact on the human psyche; but we need you to understand how confusing this can be for us.

Yes, God's kingdom is a global phenomenon, and the Master of this massive harvest may need you elsewhere at some point. Your congregation's last three pastors may have told them of Philip in Acts 8 just before they walked out the door. God needed him elsewhere and plucked him from the midst of a great revival so he could ride shotgun with an Ethiopian. Your people may know the story (too well) and may wish that their last three Philips had left *them* in the midst of revival, too. They know that God speaks to you and may, at some point, direct you elsewhere; but some of the previous departures didn't seem all that spiritual to them. Their previous pastor may have left when he was clearly angry; two others may have done so when they were invited to lead bigger churches. Another might have gone to serve closer to his wife's parents, while still another might have become a denominational leader. And all of them told this congregation the same thing—that God spoke to them and was leading them elsewhere.

Now, don't misunderstand what your people might be thinking—they believe God does that. But they'd probably feel more confident in those individual cases had their former pastors just disappeared and shown up at the next missions conference with an Ethiopian (like Philip did). Instead, it seems like God gets the credit every time a pastor leaves them—much like the boy who ends things with his girlfriend by suggesting to her that "it's simply God's will." If God has given you and your people a vision for your church, how would He let you leave before you get there? Moses crossed the whole desert with his people, even sticking with them when their lack of faith locked them in the sand. He could have moved on in frustration, but he stuck it out.

Yes, God may have a variety of plans for your life, and your time with one congregation may not fill three decades; but please understand that, if people are going to move forward with you, they need to know you're not going to disappear when the going gets a bit tough. You may lose heart when a few of them abandon the journey, but they all lose heart when you're no longer at the front of their line. And given the history of most congregations like theirs, they've probably lost such heart more than once.

You don't need a degree in Church Health and Development to know that long-term pastorates make for stronger churches. Yes, it's possible for a pastor to stay too long, but very few come close to risking that. In truth, it takes about five years for a new pastor to truly become the leader of a pre-existing congregation (one he didn't start), and the average tenure of a lead pastor typically runs about four or five years. See the problem? That's right! Just when people are about ready to start trusting their pastor, he's typically on to something else. The Jell-O of his vision has just started to harden into some new possibilities when the tasty dessert is yanked from their lips.

Here's the simple truth: for you to lead by example, they'll need you to be here. Your commitment to their future—or at least their perception of that commitment—will ultimately open the door to their level of commitment. If you're not all in, don't be surprised by your people's reluctance to invest their full hearts, energies, and finances in where you think they should go.

Of all the analogies Jesus could have used to describe the pastoral function, the shepherd is surely the most poignant. Yes, shepherds know how to manage sheep and care deeply for their wellbeing; but the most significant aspect of shepherd life is that the guy with that crooked staff isn't going anywhere. He steps up when bears attack. He comes toward the sheep when storms threaten. He moves to the front when green grass is lacking and water must be found. He never runs away! We need you to stay with us, Pastor, if we're going to understand your heart and allow it to rewrite our programming. We want to trust you, and time will allow us to do that. You don't need to tell us that you hope to someday retire here. In fact, it might be better if you didn't say stuff like that—our last three pastors said that too, and then left us around year three. Instead, stay with us through some hard times. That'll show us your determination. Stay with us when we resist you a bit. That will prove that you really love us. Stay with us when a few of your dreams seem to be failing. Then we'll trust you to help us overcome our own struggles.

You see, your presence with your people is their primary weapon against insecurity. They learn to trust God by trusting you. Yes, that may be a lot of unfair pressure for your human shoulders to manage, but they can only be excited by your words of their future if they believe that you want to live it with them. And as you live that vision every day, they discover both the "how" and "why" of living it with you. Jesus said that the Good Shepherd would give His life for His sheep—and that's just what He did. Your congregation probably won't require you to die for them, but they absolutely need you to live with them if your church will ever become the place you're convinced God wants it to be.

As long as we're thinking about showing them how to live the values that you preach, there's something else you should know about your people: *we're visual learners.* As we've already discussed, we learn much more effectively with pictures than we do with words—a fact that's also true of the people we're trying to reach together.

Now, we could attempt to grasp the science of this modern reality. Our entertainment has morphed since the days of our grandparents, who sat next to their moms and dads as they listened to the radio. In those days, only words could come into our houses. Pictures had to form in their minds if they were going to "see" anything. It's the same with books. They put pictures in books for little children, but the rest of us have always needed to work a bit harder. Today, everything comes with pictures. No more starving artists in this generation. Those who can draw, illustrate, or design are often among the most highly compensated because we simply can't function without their abilities. So, when it comes to leading people in change—and in just about everything else you want to do—you need to find a way show them.

Clearly, this shift to the visual has not only impacted entertainment. Informational disciplines like preaching and teaching have been affected as well. Pulpits used to be outposts on the vast horizon of words. As local shepherds, pastors talked to the sheep and talked to the sheep some more (some were better known for how much they talked than for what they actually said). Today, words still have a place, but they seldom get processed without pictures. Some speakers understand this and adorn large screens with the most important words in their messages. But others communicate even more effectively by shaping pictures in the heads and hearts of their listeners. Like the best of those old radio shows, they help the hearer see the action in the living color of their imaginations.

Frankly, the day of three-point outlines is hanging by a thread. Any assumption that a congregation will go home Sunday afternoon with three distinct ideas in their thoughts is more than a bit optimistic. It's the single storyline, the primary idea, the sole objective, that people will grasp. Give them three points and they'll choose which one to remember— probably the one with the best illustration.

Communicating in this generation requires a simpler approach. I've found one idea that can bring God's truth within reach. Each time I open the Bible, I hope to:

1) Tell them what it says
2) Tell them why it matters, and
3) Show them what it looks like.

One idea in three parts, not three points.

But it's that third part that's most important for our discussion here. The brilliance of Jesus' parables lay in their visual impact. I can see the sower sowing, I can picture the guy burying his talent in the dirt, I can watch the dad run toward his prodigal. Such images drive the point of their stories deep into my psyche.

> If people are going to do things differently,
> if they're going to adopt new values or
> change the patterns of their ministry,
> show them the end product. Help them
> see what a new day might look like.

As we've already said, don't expect your audience to connect the dots between your words and their actions on their own. Help them know what successful obedience looks like. Knowing I should without knowing *how* can be very frustrating; and if I face that frustration on too many Sundays, it'll stop bothering me after awhile. I'll get used to the routine of you talking, me applauding, and then returning to my normal routine unaffected. If people are going to do things differently, if they're going to adopt new values or change the patterns of their ministry, show them the end product. Help them see what a new day might look like. Paint the beautiful picture of what you've seen that they haven't yet. If they can imagine the wonders of the "Promised Land" you long for and picture themselves in the midst of such a better day, they'll understand where they're going and more enthusiastically engage in the journey.

If we can see it, maybe we can be it.

I have a somewhat ambivalent relationship with roller coasters.

My wife and I raised two sons, both of whom occasionally like to push the proverbial envelope in their entertainment choices. Any trip to an amusement park guaranteed at least one lap through the seemingly endless line for a trip on that park's most exciting ride. If it looped, if it broke speed records, or if it shot its passengers out of a cannon, my boys were ready and my wife was quick to suggest that this was an ideal opportunity for bonding with their father. *Thanks, dear. . . .*

After shuffling along with hundreds of other would-be riders, we'd finally arrive at the mouth of whatever high-tech (or no-tech) monster promised maximum thrill and bladder testing. I dutifully took my seat alongside my grinning, nearly-squealing sons, waiting for the moment my life would feel pushed to its ragged edge. Now, I'm a calm person—a dad who prides himself on maintaining composure in every circumstance. You might get a "thumbs up" or a grin out of me, but I'm no screamer; and I notice the in–flight photos at a nearby gift shop that indicate that a camera will be clicking somewhere in our death-defying journey. So I'd simply grit my teeth, pretend to be enthusiastic, and thank God that the safety bars clicked tightly into place. Here we . . . went.

As I said, my connection to such thrill rides is a bit ambivalent. I'm glad to engage such moments with my boys, and I'm glad when the little car that transported us through space reaches its parking space. I was literally just along for the ride. Just give me something to hold onto, and I'll go wherever the cables might take us. But that's the key. *Give me something to hold onto.*

In a local church's journey of change, that's what the people need. Pastor, give us handholds. Visions and dreams operate most completely in the world of ideas. Congregations grow accustomed to talk, to descriptions of the ideal and wish lists for the future. We're all about what we need to do and why we need to do it. It's just that we don't get much to hold onto—the specifics of *how* that make surviving the ride easier. Many churches engage the roller coaster of their ministry existence as though no one has locked them into their seats or shown them where to put their hands. They are propelled through eternal destinies with great energy, but the journey feels precarious because there seems to be little to hold onto. No safety bars, no clear instructions . . . just a lot of have-tos and need-tos that rarely turn into want-tos. A big part of showing us what it looks like is giving us small ways to engage the big ideas of our church's vision. I may agree and applaud the dream, but until I have some clear steps to take, I'm really not getting any closer to living it.

As a pastor amidst the wonderful congregation I previously mentioned, I had a big dream. I wanted us to be the friendliest, most genuinely engaging congregation in town (actually, in the world, but one step at a time). I could, and did, provide dozens of biblical reasons for loving people. I proclaimed such a dream with all the intensity my now 5'9" frame could muster. And I challenged a great group of people to ride this coaster with me—people who seemed to really want to climb into that car and head for great heights.

But one Sunday morning, I couldn't help but notice the wide gap between dream and reality. For all our passion and cool vision slogans, our Sunday guests stood alone during "greeting time" while our best dreamers discussed yesterday's college basketball game with each other. We had people to love right there in the room with us, but the moment slipped by nearly unnoticed.

I noticed. And in that moment, I had two options: I could either decide that we weren't committed enough to our new direction and purpose, or I could accept responsibility for failing to show my church family how to do what we said we wanted to do. The first option meant I could blame them for their lack of focus, preach a few more "we have to" kind of messages, and grade their performance on some future Sunday. After all, this day's evidence said, "We don't get it!"—or, more accurately, "*You guys* don't get it!"

But I knew that wasn't true. The guys huddled in sports discussions really wanted to reach people. They wanted our church to grow and for people to grow with it. So I took the second option, the one that put responsibility on me as their leader, and devised some practical strategy. That next week, I called together our leaders—not to berate them or show game film of their failure to be friendly last Sunday. Instead, I asked them to take a few specific steps with me. For the next six months, I asked them to commit to three unique action steps each time they attended one of our weekend services.

First, I asked them to MEET someone they had never met before: simply to find someone they'd never personally spoken with and initiate an introduction.

Second, I asked them to PRAY with someone or promise to pray for someone when they became aware of a need. In our church, we often had times of praying for one another, so this step was as simple as stepping up to put a hand on someone's shoulder, supporting them in whatever need they were currently facing. Or maybe when my team would hear that someone was facing surgery that week, they would take time to speak to this person personally and promise to pray for them on the date of their operation.

Third, I asked them to HELP someone. This was the easiest step of all. They'd just look around for someone who looked like they needed help. Maybe their arms were too full or they'd tried to manage more children than they had hands. Maybe that diaper bag looked too heavy or someone seemed a bit lost in the church hallway. Lots of people could use a little help if someone was just paying attention.

As I unpacked this three-step strategy to my group, they responded enthusiastically. I even added a little pastoral creativity, calling our new plan MPH (Meet, Pray, Help) and connected it to the more familiar phrase "miles per hour," telling them that, each time they did this, we would pick up speed in our race to become the church we wanted to be. We printed little "MPH" cards so they could record the names of those they met, prayed with, and helped each week.

I probably don't have to tell you that things changed dramatically in the next few weeks. Imagine your entire leadership team coming to church each week looking for people to meet, pray with, and help. I saw women running across the church parking lot to meet visitors who had slipped past them. There were folks praying with each other in the church hallway even before service had started. You couldn't drop a ballpoint pen without someone grabbing it before it hit the floor. Deacons were carrying diaper bags, prayer lists were growing by the minute, and guests were telling me they'd never been in a place where people were so friendly.

Yes, our church grew significantly in those six months. In fact, it kept growing, because my leaders loved the MPH experience so much that they kept it up long after we ran out of cards. But the real difference was in the leaders themselves. They began living our dream and inviting other church friends to join the fun. Their commitment to our new direction exploded, and they led our church to climb higher than any roller coaster could ever take us. All they needed was a place to grab onto. They'd known what kind of church we wanted to be and why we wanted to be that, but a few simple *hows* gave them the chance to begin living that dream.

Sometimes folks need to act their way into new thinking, and they need their pastor to show them some simple steps.

Some church folks are put off by the word "strategy." They think it doesn't sound spiritual enough. But here, we're just talking about identifying simple ways to live the purpose we like to talk about. "Just do this. . . ." helps a hope become a reality. Sometimes folks need to act their way into new thinking, and they need their pastor to show them some simple steps. Unfortunately, the change journeys in many churches crumble in frustration for both pastor and people. Pastor is disappointed that the people don't seem to be getting "it," and the people just aren't sure what to do. So Pastor, when they ask for some places to hold onto, what they're needing is clear direction. Give them something to grasp. They're excited about the ride and how amazing everything will be, but they really need somewhere to put their hands.

We hope you understand our heart. *We're with you . . . at least, we really want to be.* We're starting to see the challenges you see, and we know there's a great deal that we need to do. But we need you to connect the "why" of our collective passion to the "how" of your desired action. If you've got a picture of the desired result, that's the picture we really need to be carrying in our wallets each day.

Don't just tell us what to do, but show us what it looks like. Motivational speeches have their place. Good coaches know how to give them during pregame warmups or in locker rooms at halftime, but they also know that speeches don't replace practice time. If you don't show us what to do, we probably won't be able to connect the dots between vision and action.

Please remember that *unfair expectations work both ways.* We know we'll occasionally cross the line and want you to do more than is reasonable, but we've been on the receiving end of such unrealistic requirements, too. If you make the effort to understand where we live and what we really face each day, we'll be more likely to choose a clearer view of your challenges, too.

Pastor, we want you to stay and *we need you to stay long enough to help us reach the targeted destination.* Rome wasn't built in a day and neither was anything else that truly matters. Please don't add your name to the list of pastors who thought their role in our lives was simply to tell us what needs to happen and then move on. We need someone to live that journey with us if we're ever going to get there, and we hope that someone is you.

Don't forget that *we're visual learners.* Actions speak louder than words. If you show us what it looks like to live God's plan for our church and our individual lives, your words will even get louder in our ears.

Finally, Pastor, *give us handholds.* Turn your dream into a short list of next steps. Give us a road map to follow, and you increase the likelihood that we'll successfully make the journey. Don't just cheer us on and hand us cups of weekly water. Mark the path clearly and run the race with us. If you do, you'll increase the possibility that we'll stand together in the winner's circle someday.

CHAPTER SEVEN

PACE . . .

Perspective often drives pace . . .

arlier in this book, we made a case for allowing a change journey to move a bit more slowly than the leader might prefer. In truth, the larger the change, the more critical role that pace will play in its acceptance. But there are other factors besides speed that a leader must consider when guiding any large group through change. And perspective may well top that list.

Every seasoned leader understands that people perceive change from their own platforms. They have their own angles, shaped by their experiences and attitudes, and some are quite unafraid to share those perspectives with others—especially the one they think is "calling the shots." The issue of perspective and its impact on change took an important turn for me when I reconsidered my view of one of the Bible's great change stories. Remember Moses and his remarkable quest to lead an entire nation to new digs beyond a vast desert? Well, one day, it occurred to me that his journey wasn't truly contained in the neat, comfortable package my mind had previously created for it. As a child, my Sunday School take-home papers had always portrayed a kind of "family-picnic" aesthetic, in which smiling children played with smiling animals while moms and dads built campfires on which to cook s'mores.

One day, I realized that this march to freedom didn't look like that *at all*.

In truth, the numbers were too vast and the desert realities too intense for the attractive images my mind had borrowed from ancient flannelgraphs. You see, Moses was leading somewhere between one and three million people to their new, God-promised homes, depending on which Bible scholar you read. During one late-night discussion of these matters, a friend did a little math and told me that, even on the lower end of those numbers, such a massive group would cover miles of that desert. He said that, if you lined those people up in neat rows, ten abreast, and marched them through the sand like the British apparently marched during our Revolutionary War, the line would stretch seventy to ninety miles. Wow! Of course, things wouldn't have been nearly that orderly—not with all their possessions, the animals, and the chaotic realities that people of all ages, moving all their possessions across a desert, would bring.

But even if you could contain that herd inside a seventy-mile-long swarm, and if you could cover ten miles each day (an amazing achievement, given the conditions), there'd be about a week of travel between the guys at the front of the line and those bringing up the rear—a week!

Suddenly, I realized that—if his calculations were even close to correct— this journey would seem very different depending on where you found yourself in the line. Think about that for a moment. If you were among those near the front, chances are that the journey would be very exciting. Up front, you'd likely see Moses and the other leaders more often. You'd be among the first to hear your leader give directions, among the first to experience some of the great moments (like walking through the dry bed of the Red Sea or tasting the water that flowed from that rock), and you might think that Promised Land could be just over the next sand dune. Talk about an amazing journey! Yes, if you're up at the front, you'd likely have a very positive outlook on the changes you're experiencing. "C'mon, Moses! Let's go faster! This is great! Pass me another handful of that manna!" Little wonder you're quick to pack your belongings each morning when Moses says it's time to move forward.

Pastor, wouldn't it be great if every member of your church was that excited about the new direction you've placed before them? You might think that, given Christ's mission and the passion you have for the vision He's given you, everyone should be that excited. But the truth is that only about twenty percent of your people see this journey from a "near-the-front" perspective. Think for a moment about who, most likely, would have held those front-row tickets in Moses' journey. Wouldn't it have been folks like the leaders, the young and aggressive, and others who were most excited about where they were headed? Surely this group included those most anxious to get away from Egypt. Likely, those who had little experience with setbacks or previous hurts would rush forward, too. These are the folks who can't wait to get started on the latest change. They have little attachment to where we've been and a great desire to be somewhere else. It's an exciting group to lead because they, perhaps like Pastor, have little invested in the past and a whole lot of hope for the future. So when Pastor says, "Let's go!" this is the gang that's hard to slow down.

But everybody's not in the front with you, Pastor.

About three to four days back is another group—the folks in the middle. Now, these friends want the Promised Land too, but the journey for them is quite different than those leading the way. Three days back means you don't have much direct contact with Moses—most of your information comes secondhand. You get some of that rock water, but only by using a cup that's been passed through the ranks. Folks in the middle generally bear some frustration with the fast movers—they've been walking through their debris for a while. As they say, if you're not the lead dog, the view rarely changes. So three days back, the journey isn't as much fun. Like a car stuck in a long line of traffic, you can see how far you've got to go, and usually, you can tell that those up ahead haven't reached the destination yet.

Now, who's in the middle? About sixty percent of your congregation— that's who. Most folks live in the middle. They don't rush to the cutting edge because they've been cut a few times. They're not slackers at the back, either. These folks are just a bit more cautious. When the command comes to "move out," they don't respond immediately. These friends would like a bit more information. They've paid the price of a few past missteps and would like to be sure we're really on the right road. But they still want the Promised Land. Pastor, please remember that!

> ## Most folks live in the middle. They don't rush to the cutting edge because they've been cut a few times.

You see, often in a church's journey to a new day, those who don't immediately show enthusiasm for the new direction are labeled as the opposition. Many pastors have decided that everyone should be one of those early adopters and respond to new opportunities with enthusiasm. If you don't, you must be against the idea—and ultimately against the rest of us. So these pastors draw lines in the proverbial sand and wonder why they end up with only that front twenty percent still following them. If you treat these folks in the middle as though they're your enemies, they may actually become such. But that's not really who they are. They want the dream of a better future, but their dream button's been gummed up by a few bad experiences. They remember the last time they ran forward—no one warned them of the rocks that ultimately tripped them up. But they want to go forward, and they will soon. In fact, folks in the middle are waiting for one thing: they need to see forward movement before they'll gather their belongings and get back in line. They need to see some gains so they can more easily believe that the dream is possible. They'll go with you, but the guys in the middle never move first. We'll come back to this fact in a moment.

So far, we've discussed eighty percent of your congregation, but there are others—and you probably know exactly who they are, don't you?

Every line has a back. For Moses, this gang is about a week behind him and the other leaders. These guys are bringing up the rear, and they know it. To them, Moses is a guy they haven't seen in person since the Red Sea. In fact, the only contact this group feels to the journey is the movement of the crowd. *Where are we going? What's up ahead? When will we stop to massage our feet?* No one back here knows the answers to any of those questions. Every time these folks reach the Rest Area, the others are packing up to leave.

Life in the back of Moses' line had to be the worst of desert experiences. I'm not sure anyone would choose this spot willingly. Instead, most would feel they're victims of their circumstances—stuck at the back because they can't move quickly, they have more to carry, or no one listened when they begged the group to slow down.

Who's back here? You probably guessed: the slow movers, the less-than-energetic, and the ones with the most stuff or the least ability to carry it. Some might be aged, though I've found older saints at the front of the line in some places. These are the people who drone on with, "Are we there yet?" day after day after day. Some are a bit more attached to where we've been than where we think we're going. When the latest command to move out passes down through the ranks, these friends respond with, "Oh, c'mon, I just planted tomatoes!"

In most groups, about fifteen percent of the people occupy these spots. And, believe it or not, these friends actually want to get to the Promised Land, even though you'll seldom hear them say such a thing. They want a better future, but they typically don't believe they can get there—or they doubt there's a place for them there if they do. They usually don't doubt what the rest of us can do, but they have serious reservations about themselves. That's what their complaining is truly all about. But they can get there, and many of them will, if you genuinely love them. They'll begin to chase the vision and live new values if you don't abandon them in the desert. They'll find their way forward if they're convinced that you believe they can. And when they do, you'll know that the new vision has finally taken root.

We said that the people in the middle won't move until they see forward movement. This group at the back typically doesn't move until they're afraid of being left behind. When they see everyone else moving ahead, and when they gain confidence through your encouragement to join the rest of us, they'll drain the sand from their socks and get back in the game. I can tell you from experience that when someone in the back of our journey begins to move with us, well, there are few days that feel more wonderful.

Now, if you're good at math, you know we still have five percent of our folks wandering out there somewhere, unaccounted for. Who are they? They're the non-adopters. These are the people who hear you say that we're going "this" way and they decide to go "that" way. One of the hardest parts of leadership can be watching good friends reject your journey and go their own way. Ideally, we want the entire congregation to move toward that Promised Land with us, but some simply won't.

I can't say anything that will make those moments feel better. Yes, there are other churches, and leaving us doesn't mean they're leaving God. I know the things we tell ourselves to salve the wounds we feel, and the concern we maintain for their futures. After all, we know that life really can be a desert, and typically, those who go off on their own amidst the sand and heat don't fare too well. So we love every individual and long for each one to embrace our future together. A few may choose otherwise but, as their leader, I don't ever want to be the one who draws their line in the sand. If you love them and genuinely care for their futures, you earn the right to lead them; and that door may open again once they've worked through whatever problems they have with our map.

So when you look back across that vast wilderness and see the thousands clustered in their own perception of realities, you realize that this journey feels different for people depending on where they're at in the line. Pastor, that's why your people want you to hear them when they say, "We may not be seeing things from your same vantage point."

I hope the preceding analogy helps you gain a better understanding of the *why* behind the moments of resistance you encounter on a change journey. Remember that Moses faced quite a bit of grumbling too—you're in good company.

Perspective can be a very difficult management challenge. You see, no matter how hard you try, your people won't see their church and the great ideas you want to bring to its ministry through the lenses you're wearing. Even Jesus had a hard time getting His disciples to "lift up their eyes." Again—good company. But this discussion of perspective aims to achieve more than helping you get a handle on the complainers. In truth, Moses, you need to think through how you might drain some of the juice from your growing opposition.

First, keep in mind that *people won't embrace what they don't understand.* Surprises aren't usually well-received when they mess with our comfort. Making changes in some of the familiar elements of your church's ministry without good communication is a recipe for disaster, no matter how small the change might be. We've all heard stories of congregational battles that reached epic proportions over seemingly simple things like carpet color, organ relocation, and small alterations to the order of service. No, we shouldn't be fighting over these things; but when you fail to communicate such changes effectively, you garner disproportionate responses. After all, you're the new guy—who said you could move the organ, anyway? While manna in Moses' wilderness got a bit tiring after a while, at least the people knew where it came from and what to do with it. If I have to figure out this new stuff on my own, well, it makes sense that we're going to have a problem.

Second, *consider involving a few more people in the decision-making process.* If all the decisions seem to be coming from a single voice at the front of the line, you're helping folks focus the target of their frustrations. Include some of those "middle" people, and even a few from the rear of the journey, in the conversation. You may learn a bit about others' perspectives, and it would be great to have an ally back there, too.

Third, *be available to the whole line.* Just because the new people and the young people are more fun to run with doesn't mean they should dominate your attention. While Moses couldn't have traversed his seventy-mile line, keeping up with how everyone was doing with their piece of the journey, your line isn't that big. If you only give time to the people who love every breath you take, you'll be easily derailed by those with different feelings. Keep your ear to the ground, even if it means you might get your head stepped on a few times.

Big-time shepherds may ultimately manage major wool production, but they better not forget how to take care of sheep.

Now, there are some leadership gurus who will insist that you can't grow your organization until you limit who has access to you as the leader. Frankly, that idea has taken root within the church, even though it seems difficult to find in Scripture and doesn't connect very well to the shepherd analogy that the Good Book uses to describe servant leadership. No, we don't want to wash feet when there are strategies to build; but recheck the job description and see which one seems most critical to the Boss. Yes, an effective leader will spend most of his time developing the leaders around him. Yes, their capacity will allow us to more effectively minister to more and more people. But the key word in those sentences continues to be "most." Most is not all. Big-time shepherds may ultimately manage major wool production, but they better not forget how to take care of sheep.

To simplify, be a listener. Let those with different perspectives have opportunity to express their concerns. Sometimes, you'll be able to address those issues in a way that helps; other times, you may learn a few things that will help you lead more effectively. Wouldn't it be great if you didn't have to go fifty miles out of your way before you realize you made a wrong turn? Pastors who only listen to their friends are more likely to miss some good information coming from their supposed detractors.

Finally, the perception issue speaks of pace, too. Without question, the Promised Land is an amazing destination, and most of us would rather not linger at the rest areas along the way. But remember that there are many travelers among us who don't move as fast as you do. *Slowing down increases the likelihood that our slower-moving friends will make the journey with us.*

When we speak of perspective, our goal is to better understand the nature of the common resistances we'll encounter on this road to change—to understand so we can love. Pastor, please understand that most of our resistance is more about us than you. As we saw in the Promised Land story, those who speak most loudly against change may be unknowingly expressing their own lack of confidence that a new day is meant for them. We can see how some of Moses' crowd was afraid of the future. Slaves afraid of freedom? Yes, it happens a lot. Have you ever watched as someone who finds God's grace emerges from a tragic life of broken choices, only to drift back into those same choices and re-engage their former path to destruction? On the surface, it's truly unimaginable that a person would make such a decision, but many do—because of fear.

You see, the new path is unknown. Former ways, as bad as they were, are familiar ways. One can find himself saying, "I knew what to do there" or, "That's the only world I've ever known" as they slip back toward the edge of the cliff. New journeys seem to require a new skill set and new determination. New decision-making can feel threatening, even if the destination is heaven itself. So people tend toward what they know, regardless of the sensibleness of their choices. Why else would some Israelites want to return to Egypt?

In your journey of change, Pastor, some of us will express attitudes and ideas that make the same amount of sense to you. We may seem to prefer the ineffectiveness of the status quo over the promise of your better day, but it's not because we don't want your dream. We just lack the faith that we can get there. Other times, that resistance has grown from our past hurts and disappointments. You don't have to be punched in the nose too many times before you stop wanting to put your nose out there. Some of the arguments people make for not moving forward are little more than conjured-up excuses they believe will help them avoid more potential pain.

Perspective is usually about me.

Unfortunately, such self-focus makes the ideal partner for church decline. When what we do at church and how we do it must be aligned with my preferences and comfort, my church will struggle. Jesus established a Church that must be outward-focused—eyes on the needs of others—if it's going to be healthy.

So Pastor, if you find yourself amidst a church in decline, you're likely leading people with eye (or "I") problems. Like the ancient gang that populated Moses' trek across the sand, their attitudes toward the journey are primarily influenced by how the path feels to them, not by the beauty of where they're going or the brilliance of the plan to get us there.

So how does resistance affect movement? One thing your people need you to know about making change is that we need you to move forward . . . just don't leave us too far behind. In our Promised Land analogy, we noted that about twenty percent of the people are typically ready to move forward when you first present the plan. These are the Early Adopters, and they are likely both excited and determined to take these positive steps with you. But, as we also noted, not everyone shares their enthusiasm.

Remember those Mid-Adopters. Yeah, that's the big bunch—they comprise about sixty percent of your congregation. These friends want the wonderful future you describe. They're heavily invested in your local church, and talk of a new, more effective day stirs them inside, too. But they aren't ready to move just because you said, "Let's go!" Still, they will move. We've already said that these folks move when they see forward movement. So that means you're going to have to take a few steps forward to encourage them. They need to see some progress, some legitimate evidence that the new path you've chosen will lead toward your congregation's goals, and then you can expect them to join in.

As a leadership challenge, this can become a bit tricky. You need to move forward, but you can't move too fast. If you don't make some progress, the Mid-Adopters will never move; but if you change too much, you'll make the gap between you and them too wide to effectively lead them. This gap is managed safely by making your first change steps small ones. Don't roll out the big transitions first. Make small changes they can be excited about. Go ahead and paint that restroom, make the bulletin more attractive, and add a few quality touches to the worship services. Take steps that can build a stronger sense of pride in your church's ministry.

Don't begin the journey with its most controversial pieces. If you're pastoring a traditional church, changing the music style isn't a smart way to announce a change journey. Don't cancel a service or disband a popular Sunday School class. Choose easy steps as first steps until you can gain the involvement of a bit more than those front twenty percent.

Don't roll out the big transitions first. Make small changes they can be excited about.

You may argue that the major changes are the key to your ultimate ministry success—and I won't disagree. But new music amidst a fighting congregation won't help you reach more people for Jesus. People can tell when they've entered a room where conflict stirs below the surface. They can sense it and smell it, even if folks try to keep it hidden. Ever stopped by to visit a friend and discover that you inadvertently interrupted a marriage argument? They'll smile at you, but you can tell that stuff's going on. If you take big, controversial change steps too early in the journey, you'll likely create the aroma of conflict in your beautiful sanctuary. Start with the easy stuff and celebrate the results.

Now, while making small initial changes can frustrate aggressive pastors, moving forward when some aren't yet on board raises concern for others. "Consensus" leaders are most comfortable when they feel that everyone is comfortable with every step they take. They prefer unanimity before action and spend a lot of energy trying to accommodate and adjust their steps to keep everyone happy. Such a mentality may please the congregation, but it achieves very little progress. The "consensus" approach almost guarantees that minority opinions will keep the church paralyzed, especially when those opinions favor the status quo. If Moses hadn't moved until everyone was ready, he'd still be on the far bank of the Red Sea.

When you understand that most people need to see evidence of forward movement before moving, you realize how important these early steps really are. So to move at the best pace, your goal must be to elevate the feelings your people have about their church. As you make small, even cosmetic-type changes, you don't risk major conflict and you can increase the good feelings in the room. And don't forget that a part of your battle is helping your Late Adopters—that fifteen percent lingering at the back—believe that they can be a part of the future, too. When you make the first steps simple, you increase their confidence that the future can include them.

If you trace Moses' steps across that wilderness, you'll find that he and God didn't choose the straightest available path for the wilderness journey. Instead, they took a bit of a circuitous route, avoiding some battles the people were incapable of winning. If Moses would have taken the direct path, most of his people wouldn't have been able to survive the journey. Few mountain roads follow a straight path up the hill. Instead, most paths circle the mountain as they climb, making the journey easier on your mode of transportation. In the same way, taking achievable steps first avoids a straight climb to your destination, instead finding a path that more of your people can engage with you. Yes, the smoother path will take a bit longer; but you don't want to reach the summit and discover that you're all alone.

One other element of pace is time. Frankly, Pastor, while your people want a great future for their local church, they want you to know that their lives are quite full and, well . . . this isn't their full-time job.

Modern schedules continue to be more and more crowded. A few of us remember the days when people thought that advancing technology would fill our lives with more leisure time (it's hard not to chuckle as I write that). Truth is, every time-saver creates the expectation of greater productivity. Because individual tasks have been made simpler and faster, more tasks have been added. The "all" of getting it all done is a much bigger pile than before. So there are more work meetings and longer hours at the office. Many chase extra income with "side hustles" made necessary by spiraling living expenses and the desire to maintain lifestyles once more easily afforded. Kids' schedules make time management a challenge for today's twelve-year-olds. Families have spread out across the country and travel options have increased, making weekend trips to maintain connections routine. Add it all together, and the average parishioner is typically too busy to give the number of volunteer hours that once marked their spiritual expression.

For pastors, the result often feels like a diminishing level of commitment. Churches that once knew their most dedicated members by their attendance at two or three services each week now wrestle with those who consider themselves deeply involved even though they darken the church door only a couple of times each month. You might think this would free pastors to pursue their change agendas more freely, but usually, the opposite is true. Where a single Sunday School teacher might have held down the fort fifty weeks a year in the past, today three or four are needed to fill slots in a rotating schedule that can accommodate their availability. Church leaders are so busy keeping the status quo adequately staffed that there is less time to pursue new ideas.

And there's one group that still has nearly as much time as before: the elder saints, many of which are most tied to the way things have been. Pastors find that those most interested in change tend to be the least available to help it happen. So the change team becomes "those people" to the rest of the congregation: "those people" who don't seem to be around as much as the rest of us. "Why are we doing things their way, anyway?"

Finding a new day in a local congregation requires time and hard work. Change always demands additional effort, and if the people we need are too busy, more of the load falls to the pastor. At least Moses had everyone's undivided attention. He didn't have to carry other people's luggage. Getting through that wilderness was everyone's full-time job. I'm guessing no one's cell phone rang during the whole trip!

Now, this lack of available time doesn't mean that people don't care about where their church is headed. They do, but pastor quickly discovers that the ideas and priorities that govern every day of his week only fill his peoples' windshields a few hours each week. "Sorry, Moses, I can't leave for Kadesh-Barnea quite yet. I've gotta work this weekend."

The issue of time affects pace in that a pastor must adjust his expectations to match the availability of his people. He can't expect his people to maintain a deep focus on the church's vision when they're also chasing a corporate vision all week long. Now, don't lose hope. Just realize that the speed of your journey will be affected by the level of focus your congregation can maintain. If they can't keep up with your full-time pace, they'll either find another, slower journey or become more attracted to the status quo.

So when a pastor leads change, the necessary pace will almost always be slower than he or she prefers. As we have seen, that pace is determined by perception, resistance, and the available time your people have to work with you.

Here's what we need you to know: *We may not be seeing things from your vantage point.*

Perspective is an individual experience. Each member of your church will experience the change journey from where they stand. They'll never share the view you enjoy from behind that pulpit. Some will walk up front, just a few steps behind you. These folks will share your enthusiasm, applaud your vision, and respond quickly to the shifts in direction you know are necessary. But most of the congregation stands back a bit. They aren't as quick to respond, often because of past experiences, present comforts, or simply a more cautious approach to life. These Mid-Adopters want a great future, just like your more aggressive friends, but they need to see some positive steps before they gain the confidence to fully join in. And there's a group that moves even more slowly. These Late Adopters tend to have more invested in where we've been than where you think we may be going, and they may lack confidence that your preferred future will have a place for them. They hear your dreams and see the excitement of others, but they remember past failures and aren't certain that they have the strength for the necessary path.

So Pastor, keep in mind that each church member has his place in this line. If you're going to help everyone move forward, you'll probably need to broaden your perspective to include some understanding of life further back. Don't make the mistake of interpreting slow movement as resistance, but instead allow room for some to hold a different view of your changes.

Remember that *people won't embrace what they don't understand*. Communication is critical to a successful journey. Don't think that the best information will get passed through the ranks with the same accuracy and enthusiasm you hope for.

Don't make the mistake of interpreting slow movement as resistance, but instead allow room for some to hold a different view of your changes.

It may help if you consider *involving a few more people in the decision-making process*. Once you realize that Mid-Adopters and Late Adopters comprise nearly three-fourths of your congregation, it makes sense to be sure some of these are a part of your strategic team. Don't just hang out with the change mavens. Balance the input you receive by listening to those who want your great future but who feel a need to move more slowly.

On that same front, it will help if you can *be available to the whole line*. Moses was leading well over a million people, so hearing from all camps wasn't achievable. But, assuming your congregation is a bit smaller, it seems likely that you can find ways to stay connected with both the fast-moving and those who respond more slowly. Oftentimes, people will make a better effort to move forward if they believe you've listened and understand the difficulties they encounter with each step.

Ultimately, perspective informs pace by convincing a leader that *slowing down will increase the likelihood that our slower-moving friends will make the journey with us*. Please don't leave people in the desert! If adjusting the pace will allow more members of your congregation to be a part of the future, isn't that adjustment worth it?

As we said, *most of our resistance is more about us than you*. Past hurts, lacking confidence, and not always understanding where we're going or why we're trying to get there form the core of resistance to change. People may argue with your ideas or act as though their difficulty with change is more your problem than theirs, but the truth is that many have issues standing between them and their ability to embrace hope for a new future—both for their church and also for their individual lives. As a pastor, you know to manage that knowledge with love and understanding. After all, caring for weaknesses of the sheep is a huge part of the shepherd's job description.

Amidst this sea of Early, Mid, and Late Adopters, your congregation *needs you to move forward, just don't leave them too far behind*. You can't wait until everyone's ready to move—that's a day that won't come, and those ready for change will move on without you at some point. So a pastor has to manage pace by taking easy steps first. This will allow many people to gain confidence in the forward movement and join in more quickly. Don't start with your most controversial or complicated moves. Take simple steps, and soon you'll have enough people moving to begin engaging the bigger challenges.

Finally, your people need you to remember that *this isn't their full-time job*. Demanding schedules and competing commitments will affect the time your people can give to your new ideas. And that will ultimately impact how rapidly you can move forward. Our lack of availability may tempt you to try and do everything, but that's not the answer, is it? Instead, take things a bit more slowly so we can join you in giving our best to our church's future.

Never forget that the goal isn't just to achieve a greater future for our church. The real goal is that we find that future together so we can experience it and enjoy it just as we've dreamed. For that to happen, it's quite likely that the pace will need to slow down a bit.

CHAPTER EIGHT

PARTNERSHIP . . .

Pastor, there's one more thing your people really want you to know . . .

You see, they may not talk about it much, but many of your people know the pressure you feel to help their church become something it's never been—or maybe something it's struggled to be. They have some understanding of the expectations you feel—not just the ones they exert, but those from your peers and the leaders that monitor the church's progress under your leadership.

They also have some idea of the stories you hear: the tales of great churches and the equally-great pastors who lead them. They likely understand if, in a random corner of your heart, there's a desire to be one of those guys. Even though the people of your church don't engage the challenges of the church every day like you do, they know about longing for success and wanting to make an impact because they feel those things too, even if they don't immediately associate such thoughts with the church. As we have said, there can be a natural disconnect between the dreams a congregation might have for their pastor and the ones that fill the pastor's sleepless nights. The people want a shepherd to care for them, minister effectively to their needs, and give appropriate leadership to their spiritual growth. Pastor, on the other hand, tends to steer his primary aim at building a great church: one that includes those who haven't yet walked through the doors. While people and pastor will quickly acknowledge the importance of the other's agenda, they tend to maintain their different view of the main thing.

But while this differing sense of the ideal can be frustrating and even spawn an occasional argument or two, there's no reason it should lead to an unhappy marriage, or a divorce. In fact, there's usually enough common ground to be found that people and the pastor can flourish together, provided they hold tightly to one simple idea—*we can be a team*!

Partnership is possible. In fact, it is both preferred and the only way we can navigate the road of change ahead. If you try to implement change without including us, you'll fail just as colossally as if we try to bring change without your input. But together, we can actually do this, and do it very well.

There's a lot of literature and more than a few joke books that have been written about the stubbornness of church people when it comes to facing change. We've heard about the carpet color fights and the tales of insisting that, "If the organ was good enough for the Apostle Paul ..." These stories underscore the extreme silliness of some church conflicts. Most of us know that the King James Version doesn't predate King James. The overwhelming majority of church people don't resist change in such nitpicking ways, and it's unfortunate when such perceptions are widely applied. Just because some guy called technical support when he thought the CD drive in his computer was a cup holder doesn't mean every individual that's currently unpacking a new laptop is a moron.

If a pastor can lay aside the caricatures of status-quo fiends that are often drawn to audiences of certain seminars, he'll find that there are many potential partners for change amidst his current congregation. These are the folks who've heard dozens of sermons on making disciples, reaching the unconverted, and loving their neighbor. It seems safe to assume that they've taken many of those messages to heart and are just waiting to discover the necessary steps to turn sermons into actions steps. These are the people who ignore caricatures of guys like you, too. They turn away from those pictures of pastors who only care about younger people, or who only want to be a megachurch, or who think that only music that rattles light fixtures can appeal to a modern generation. They don't see you as the nickel-collecting, nose-counting, ego-driven tyrant that's often associated with church growth priorities. They want to make a difference in this community too, and you'll find in them the potential for a great and lasting partnership.

So these people have made a choice. They've decided to take some of the weight off your shoulders by joining your team. They know that, by yourself, you'll take all the hits, so they're willing to deflect as much of the shrapnel as possible and be a part of their church's solution. With a partnership, your plans have a real future—one that these people have a genuine stake in, just like you.

Pastor, the idea of partnership with your people in the journey of change implies another fact that those people want you to know: *we can help you figure this out.*

Every church has its own unique capacity and identity. There's simply nothing cookie-cutter about the local church. In spite of dozens of conferences and thousands of books that describe the wisdom and ways of the successful, you simply can't "plug and play" one pastor's idea into another congregation. Those with a few conference notebooks on their shelf have figured this out.

Now today, we often hear about congregational DNA, and there's much confidence placed in system approaches to ministry. Yes, a church can open another location and do things the way they're done at the main location, finding some measure of repeatable success. But that success hinges largely on the idea of one congregation reproducing, or recreating, itself in another. Same pastor, same leadership team, and same methodologies can often yield some of the same results.

Things don't always work out that way, but the possibility of one set of ideas working well in a similar location is a bit like trying to raise children that look and act alike. Suppose you discover a particularly brilliant and good-looking child and decide that you'd like to see more such children produced—maybe even produce one yourself (okay, this analogy will get a bit weird, but follow me anyway). My wife and I once had a woman at church tell us that she hoped her soon-to-be-born son would be just like one of our boys. She even gave him the same first name, which we decided was more of an honor than a creepy idea. Of course, you can guess the result. Her son is a fine boy with excellent qualities, of which she and her husband can be especially proud. But the first name is just about all he has in common with our boy. She and her husband didn't and couldn't have reproduced our son, no matter how hard they tried. By the way, they didn't try because that would be weird (and they're not).

So if you want to create another child to match the one who's impressed you, the best plan would be to find the original parents of that first child and ask them to recreate their environment and parenting practices. The likelihood that they can reproduce an exact copy seems limited, but if anyone has a chance, it would probably be them, right? The sometimes-surprising miracle of twins always requires the same parents. Every set shares the same mother and father. Kids who look alike are usually cut from the same parental cloth, too. So if you want a boy who looks like his older brother, your best approach would be to engage the participation of the same parents. Even then, a fair amount of uniqueness will likely emerge, but your odds of similar results are higher if the same folks are the ones producing both children.

In the same way, when the same pastor seeks to reproduce his ministry ideas in a second congregation, the odds of success are greater for him than for some of us other "parents." You see, we're not him, we're not where he's at, and we're not working with the people who have been helping him. Everything is different, meaning that his ideas and approach have a different potential in our setting. So if you want to find the best route for change in your local church, you first must realize that there's no exact script that can help you get the results that someone else is currently enjoying. Even though you can benefit from the insights they've gained on their journey, it's not their path you want or have any real chance of walking.

Pastor, if none of us have been where we're going, why not work together to find the way?

But there is a unique, dynamic reality for your congregation. God's amazing creativity has designed a tailor-made journey for you and your congregation. That's why your people want you to know that they can help. You see, they know more about being who they are than anyone else. Could there be any group of folks more aware of where they've been and what it felt like to be there? The roads attempted, insights gained, mistakes made, and any other items potentially recorded in their journey log are right there, inside the heads and hearts of those who currently fill your pews. They can help, they *want* to help, and they're likely the best help you'll ever find.

So this partnership possesses critical possibilities.

Too often, a pastor of a struggling church will decide that, since this church isn't where it needs to be, no one in the church has a clue as to what we should do. It's the ol' "they-haven't-done-it-without-me-so-I-need-to-do-it-for-them" line of reasoning. Of course, when pastors think that way, they forget that they haven't been on the needed road of success for this congregation, either. Pastor, if none of us have been where we're going, why not work together to find the way? In a journey of change, when people work in partnership with their pastor, the road gets a lot smoother. More insights are brought to the table, more gifts are available for use, and more voices can sing the rejoicing tunes of victories when we feel we're contributing to the journey.

No, the deacons may have never been to Bible college, and they may have not read the latest church growth books. Their knowledge of church growth ideas may be dwarfed by your own and they may not be able to quote the latest leadership mantras. But they have a collection of knowledge you lack, too. They know the current realities better than you do, and they've been interacting with those who feel them for many years. They've "been there and done that" an awful lot in those years when you hadn't "been there" yet.

If the path to our best future is the destination on our treasure map, wouldn't it help to have a few more minds interpreting the clues?

And Pastor, don't forget that partnership increases speed. If we're on board together, we can move a bit more quickly than we'll be able to if you're always needing to convince us of next steps. When we get to contribute to the plan, we'll feel an ownership in the new direction and give our best to helping you chase down our ideas.

A few chapters ago, we discussed the importance of a pastor's longevity if he's going to earn the right to really lead us into the future. Well, that idea of longevity brings up something else that people really want their pastor to know: *Pastor, we're in this for the long haul.*

While pastors tend to come and go every handful of years (on average), the majority of people aren't quite so mobile. Pastors often speak of how easily people just quit, abandoning years of involvement and investment for the greener pastures they think are just down the street. But such transitiveness isn't really that common. Yes, people change churches and, as a wise friend once observed, "The automobile is here to stay," which makes such moves feasible. But usually, the transient folks have their own pattern established. Those most likely to leave a church in frustration over ministry decisions tend to be those who walked in the door over something similar at their last church. Just because these "church hoppers" demonstrate a level of commitment that's barely negligible doesn't mean that the rest of your people will leave as easily. In fact, for many of them, the choice to leave their church for another is harder than changing jobs and nearly as gut-wrenching as a family breakup. They aren't going any-where—at least not until they've run through all other options.

That commitment is good news for the pastor, who wants to partner with his people in the pursuit of change. Pastor, you don't have to worry about them running out on you. Frankly, they have more right to be concerned about *your* stick-to-itiveness. Being in it for the long haul means they will prove dependable and that they can endure a few mistakes along the way. We don't have to be perfect to thrive together, but we do need to be together.

Maybe a sports analogy can add to the point. Most major sports teams benefit greatly from longevity in the locker room. When a football team's offensive line has been together for a while, their quality significantly improves. The more that basketball players play together, the better they get, because they more easily anticipate each other's abilities and moves.

Assemble a team of superstars and they'll usually struggle at first, trying to figure out how to play together. That's why the teams with the most money don't win every championship. They struggle just like other squads, because talent is only part of the equation. And if the folks at the local church keep working toward the same scoreboard, in time, they'll get better at their game, too. They want you to know that you can keep penciling their name in on the lineup card. You see, this is their church, and they're not going anywhere.

There's one more thing people want their pastor to know as they move toward change—*they really want this relationship to last.*

Pastoral transitions are difficult for most congregations. Those who have a congregational form of government know all too well the amount of work required to fill a pastor's shoes, even for a few months. And the stress of trying to get the right pastor to lead the church has its ups and downs. Those with a more ecclesiastical governance model may have a state officer choose their pastors for them, but the stress of making things work with a new leader isn't easy—especially if neither you nor your new pastor had much input in the decision. Changing a few things around the church is hard enough. Changing the name on the Pastor's study is even harder.

No one really wins if pastor doesn't stay, and real partnership demands that he does.

Unfortunately, some congregations develop a high turnover rate in their pastoral office. Usually, the more unhealthy the congregation, the less patience pastor and people will show for one another. But sending a pastor away seldom solves anything. In fact, though there aren't many studies available to prove the point, observation says that a congregation who dismisses their pastor likely won't fully recover from that choice for a decade or more. Maybe somebody should do that study and share the results with a few congregations. But the point is that no one really wins if pastor doesn't stay, and real partnership demands that he does. Whatever the process that brings a pastor to lead a local congregation, both pastor and people want to believe that God has ordered that process and generated His preferred result.

So Pastor, resist the idea that people are looking to rid themselves of you. Sure, there are some extreme cases where this may prove true. But absent a petition that accidentally lands on your desk or the announcement of a congregational meeting that you're not invited to, it's best to think better thoughts. If conflicts have escalated into divorce proceedings, things must have gone wrong somewhere, because no congregation hires a pastor with the initial hope of firing him. Laying aside the realities of a handful of really unhealthy churches, let's consider the lion's share of the bunch: these people want you to be their pastor, and they're hoping you'll lead them into the future effectively. Not only are they hoping for that, but they really believe you're the leader they need.

Sadly, churches who have dismissed a pastor tend to develop a "hired hand" idea that corrupts the role of pastor for a few years. If your congregation had to remove their last pastor, they may be susceptible to seeing you as "the guy we hired," especially if the previous removal was a congregational idea and not the result of the pastor's misconduct. When we think we hired our pastor, you can see how we might have forgotten that he serves at God's initiative. But absent a tragic story like this in recent years, the congregation will view their pastor as God's man for the job. They may even have confirmed such with their own vote. So you can see that the makings of a partnership are fully in place. They plan on staying and they really want you to stay. Now, we just have to figure out what we can do while we're spending these years together.

If we're going to achieve an effective partnership between pastor and people, what must these two differently-motivated parties bring to the table? Yes, motives are different. We've already discussed how pastor is often a bit more focused on people yet to be reached, while the congregation tends to lean toward a pastor caring for *them*. These are the two sides of the pastoral assignment coin. Both are critical and need attention. Whether you're looking at the "heads" or "tails" side, it's still the same coin. But that different focus means the relationship can be ripe for misunderstandings and frustrations. To overcome these dysfunctional moments, the pastor-and-people relationship requires three things: passion, patience, and love.

Apathy is the death knell for a congregation. People who attend church only when they feel like it seldom show up when they're apathetic. They don't make much effort and don't seem to care when things aren't going particularly well. Very few people stay in a church long enough to hate it, but apathy is an available option—especially when there's so much else in life to care about.

Passion is the antithesis to apathy. Yes, we must learn to care about the same things if we're going to get along well, but *caring* is a critical first step. When what we're doing as a congregation really matters to people, exciting things can happen. Of course, the weekly routine can work against passion. As you may have noticed, Sunday comes around every seven days, and with it comes the patterns we've developed, the familiar ways we function—things that sometimes grow so common to us that they lose their impact. As a kid, my family's faithfulness to church meant that I participated in a minimum of two hundred celebrations of the Lord's Supper, observed hundreds of baptisms, and sang my way through the hymnal enough that I can quote all four verses of most of the songs written by Fanny Crosby—Isaac Watts, too. When the routine becomes routine, apathy isn't far off.

So each of us must stir our own hearts with the mission God has placed before us. The ministry of our church must matter greatly to any who would be a member of the partnership needed to move forward. Pastor may have more opportunities to demonstrate his passion. After all, he has most of the speaking parts in each Sunday's production. But a similar, if quieter, passion must reside in the people's hearts if they will be adequate partners in pursing the future.

Patience will matter, too.

Frankly, none of us are even close to what God will one day help us become. We don't have all the answers on our first day at the table, and we'll still be missing a few when our last day comes. God does His best work in us over time, and that means our efforts to be more like Him will always be a work in progress. So yes, we want to show some progress; but there's ample reason for us to deal with each other kindly as godliness grows slowly within.

Pastor, remember that Moses was eighty years old when he finally stepped into God's full plan for his life. And he wasn't fully ready for that, nor had he become the leader he would ultimately be. Don't let the expectations of your pastor friends or even those you perceive coming from the latest ministry success stories teach you to be impatient with your people. Sheep seldom do well when they are driven hard. They do better when they're led. Pushing them from behind is likely messy work.

If pastor demonstrates patient support of those he leads . . . well, those he leads are more likely to return the favor. In spite of some moments that may imply otherwise, people don't expect their pastor to be perfect. But if you're frequently magnifying their weaknesses, they'll be glad to highlight a few of yours too.

Sheep seldom do well when they are driven hard. They do better when they're led.

Patience and passion aren't easy friends. Sometimes, our desire to fulfill the mission can tempt us to treat people as tools for getting things done rather than the *reason* for which we do them. If you have any goal that can't be achieved by loving people every step of the way, you're probably racing down a wrong path.

Love is the local church's reason for being. As we know, Jesus gave renewed focus to the idea of loving one another, making it the "new" command He would leave with His disciples. God himself had gone through the trouble of coming to earth to show us what it means to love, and then He gave the effort to follow that example, the pre-eminent place among His commands for His people.

Every now and then, it's good to remind ourselves of what love is. According to the Apostle Paul,

> *Love is patient, love is kind. It does not envy, it does not boast, it is not proud. It does not dishonor others, it is not self-seeking, it is not easily angered, it keeps no record of wrongs. Love does not delight in evil but rejoices with the truth. It always protects, always trusts, always hopes, always perseveres.*

Truth is, the apostle didn't write that for wedding ceremonies. He wrote it to a church that needed to be reminded that being super spiritual wasn't really all that impressive if they couldn't love each other when they opened their eyes. Ultimately, the Bible's best definition of love might be "self-sacrifice." Love is evident when I lay myself down for others, putting their needs ahead of my own. In this partnership we're building, that means pastor won't see caring for his congregation as a distraction from his mission, but rather as a large part of the mission itself. And the people will see their own assignment as including a servant posture toward the needs of their God-appointed shepherd. As in marriage, when we put the other's needs ahead of our own, a miraculous union begins to form.

So when you look out at those cherub-like faces each Sunday, I hope you can see some of the potential behind their tired eyes. Those folks want to be a team with you as their leader. They have so much to offer the path ahead. Many of them have history on their side. They have knowledge, insights, and experiences that your seminary training or your last church didn't provide. And *they really want to help.* The people of your congregation really want a stronger future for your church, and some of them have enough experience under this roof— or even others—to help you figure out some of the steps your church needs to take. Don't ignore their ideas or exclude them from the conversation. Just because their church needs to change doesn't mean they don't have ideas about how that can be done.

Pastor, don't forget that, in spite of a few folks who may occasionally bounce from one congregation to another, *most of us are going to be here for the long haul.* We don't change churches easily and certainly don't want to be given any reason to start that habit. We hope to build an effective ministry partnership with you because we really want our church to fulfill its mission. We don't want to live in futility and mere religious habit any more than you want to lead it.

So *we really want this relationship to last.* We don't think you became our pastor by accident. Instead, we know that our congregation is a part of Jesus' Church, and we're confident that He led you here, no matter what that process might have looked like. We believe that you're God's assigned leader for our congregation and we're ready to work with you to find the road to a healthier church.

We pledge our passion, our patience, and our love, confident that you bring those same things to us. We don't expect you to be perfect, and we're going to need a little room to miss the mark at times, too. But together, we can find a great future.

So . . . can we be partners?

EPILOGUE . . .

For several years, I've been privileged to look out my window with the condition of today's local congregations as the primary view. I've met hundreds of pastors and thousands of those who sit tuned to their ministry frequencies each week. And frankly, my respect and admiration for both groups has risen nearly every time I open my window blinds.

Pastors are amazing people, so deeply committed to one of life's most challenging career choices. They long to make a difference—not simply as a response to their own emotional needs or out of a hunger for self-worth. They give their very best to their churches because they love the One who called them to such service. It's His eternal agenda that drives them, and letting Him down seems well beyond unacceptable.

I've found congregation members to be pretty amazing too. As stated at the beginning of this book, I've peeked behind the curtain of those stories that paint church folks as "giant-headed" monstrosities with loud voices demanding adherence to the status quo, and I've found much smaller heads and kinder voices. They aren't what some of us pastors have said they are.

Together, I see amazing potential. I daydream of those moments when great pastors and great people find ways to be great together. I even get to live a few of those moments when I'm in a room where light bulbs come on and reveal the doorways to effective paths forward. Those moments are extraordinary. They have a way of crumbling the fears and frustrations that have followed some local churches for decades. Good people with a big God can do remarkable things.

And they really need to.

The wider view out my window isn't too encouraging. Literally thousands of local churches are bouncing against the rocks. They seem at risk to break up at any moment, or simply to drift away with a purposeless current. Most denominations report that four of every five churches are stuck on those rocks or slowly sinking beneath the waves. Those groups who boast that one-third of their churches are still growing don't really have anything to boast about. Like the healthiest patient in the Intensive Care Unit, they still need some serious intervention to get healthy.

Something has to change . . . and someone has to find a way to change it.

That's what this book has been about. While there are perhaps hundreds of books that will help you achieve organizational change, there aren't too many written for the unique realities of the local church, and even fewer that are written from the perspective of the people being changed. This has tried to be one of those very few.

You see, Pastor, the art and science of leading change can't be navigated by textbook ideas alone. In fact, your greatest resource for changing your church will prove to be the people riding on your ship. They may not have gotten this boat off of those rocks on their own, but they are surely a bunch of willing hands with a lot of reasons to help you as you try.

Throughout this book, we've suggested that there are several things your people want you to know before you try to lead them in change. The point of such a list isn't to suggest that you disagree with these things, distrust your people, or think that they're wearing the most frightening of Halloween masks. I know you love them, but some of the stories you've heard from other pastors may have skewed your expectations a bit.

Now that we've come to the end of this book, I see that we've suggested thirty-seven things your people want you to know. Honestly, when I started writing, I thought there might be about eight things on this list, but, as usual, your people proved to know even more than I thought.

Here's the list:

When we started together, we may not have wanted the same things.
We really want the same thing you do, even if we
might want it for different reasons.
We're going to need time to learn to trust you.
Time is actually your friend.
We actually want to trust you.
We'll go where you go if you'll come where we are.
You've missed a lot. This story started before you got here.
Yours isn't our first vision.
No matter where you think we are, getting this far hasn't been easy.
We need you to be gentle when discovering and discussing our failures.
We hope you'll walk in our old shoes a bit before
thinking we can run in your new ones.
We're not your last church or the church you've read about.
There are just some things we really weren't made to do.
It will help if you can make your plans fit what we can do.
We're probably a little confused about the vision.
We're going to need you to reinforce our grasp of what is truly important.

Don't forget that values can be really difficult to change.
We'll more likely act our way into new thinking
that think our way into new actions.
We'll need you to live those values with us.
Don't just tell us what to do, but paint us pictures of what it looks like.
Unfair expectations work both ways. We know we
do it to you and sometimes you do it to us.
We need you to stay long enough to help us reach the targeted destination.
We're visual learners (we learn best by watching you).
We need you to give us handholds.
We may not be seeing things from your same vantage point.
People won't embrace what they don't understand.
You'll get better results if you involve a few more
people in your decision-making process.
You'll need to be available to the whole line, not
just those with you at the front.
Slowing down increases the likelihood that our
slower-moving friends will make the journey with us.
Most of our resistance is more about us than you.
We need you to move forward, just don't leave us too far behind.
This isn't our full-time job.
We want to be a team.
We really want to help.
Most of us are going to be here for the long haul.
We really want this relationship to last.
We pledge to you our passion, our patience, and
our love, and those will be easier to see
when you will bring those same things to the table for us.

Wow! That's a lot that they're asking you to know or consider, isn't it? But I hope you can see the amazing potential just on the other side of such knowledge. Healthy churches find healthy paths when they're pursuing change—and that's the real goal, isn't it? I mean, if you get to the future and have no one to share it with, or if you've strewn the road with broken relationships along the way, will it really be the future you want?

Sheep and their shepherd are designed to share an extraordinary bond. And they're both really in search of some good green grass and a few refreshing streams. If sheep could talk, maybe they'd say, "Let's go find some of that together ..."

Maybe that's what *Baaa!* has meant all along.